Better Homes and Gardens

MEAT COOK BOOK

MEREDITH PRESS

New York   Des Moines

Meat makes the meal

Chances are you think first of meat in planning a meal. Each day you're faced with which cut to choose, how much to buy, how to cook it. Meat is money, too, so learn to shop the meat case wisely. If it's steak you're buying, know which type and how thick. If the budget is at low ebb, remember there's a world of good eating in bargain buys—and the food value is exactly the same.

Meat is likely to be the part of the meal you have the most questions about. That's why *Better Homes and Gardens* is bringing you a Meat Cook Book. We feel fortunate to have had Thora Hegstad Campbell, well-known home economist and meat specialist, help us compile the *Better Homes and Gardens* information.

You'll find our book packed with more than 400 recipes— each rated excellent by our Tasting Test Kitchen staff. Along with easy, skip-a-step recipes, there are family favorites— elegant entrees for company. Dozens of glamour photographs show you ways to serve meat attractively. How-to pictures help you zip through special techniques.

We hope as you thumb the pages of this Meat Cook Book, you'll get inspiration to serve a different meat every day.

A masterpiece—thick sirloin broiled to perfection; see page 23

Contents

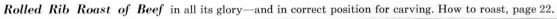

Pork Steaks with Apple Stuffing. Lots of good eating in bargain pork steaks. See page 42 for recipe.

Rolled Rib Roast of Beef in all its glory—and in correct position for carving. How to roast, page 22.

Meat favorites— a preview of what's ahead

Barbecued Ribs—a specialty of any house! These have wonderful flavor— grill ribs over coals, brush with a zesty sauce. Last half hour, peg on lemon and onion slices, toss damp hickory onto fire—pinch up foil cap over the ribs.

Chuck-wagon Beans are full of long-cook flavor—but you get a head start with canned pork and beans. (Recipe, page 120.) Bury pot in coals 6 to 8 hours, or uncover last few hours and smoke on grill—hood down.

Chef's Salad Bowl. Dad, here's a salad to make you famous! Ham and cheese team up with asparagus spears, peas, and deviled eggs on greens. Dressing can be easy shake-up kind. (How-to, page 127.) Go-withs: Hot tomato bouillon and toasted garlic bread.

Hamburger Pie, Onion Biscuits. No ordinary meat pie this! "Filling" is ground beef, canned green beans, and whole kernel corn in a jiffy, tomato-soup sauce. Doughnuts, "holes" (really biscuits seasoned with onion and celery seed) make the topper. Good family fare—speedy, too. How to make it? Turn to page 115.

Roast Turkey. Any day can be a holiday—now you can buy this bird all year round! Choose a big 25-pounder, or a petite 8-pounder. And don't overlook the convenient frozen stuffed turkeys. You'll find turkey cut-ups, too— drumsticks, wings, and quarter roasts.

We talk turkey in our poultry chapter. There are brand-new ways to serve turkey along with the good old stand-bys.

Baked Ham all decked out with fruit! A buffet natural, ham is as delicious as it is handsome. There's nothing to the fixing! Just baste with Honey Glaze during baking. (See page 45.)

Flowers of canned peach slices and maraschino cherries are the festive trim. Platter partners are lush peach halves and fluffs of parsley.

Meat buying and storage

Don't let the meat case baffle you. Take advantage of the advertised bargains . . . be adventuresome in trying new cuts. Remember, *every cut and kind of meat contains the same high quality protein.* So any meat, regardless of price, spells good nutrition . . . treat it right, and it spells good meals!

Some fresh meats are marked with a government grade. These denote quality in this order: U.S. Prime, U.S. Choice, U.S. Good. In addition, most meats carry a brand name label—the name of a packer or market. Learn the grade or brand you like best, then stick to it! Only an expert can judge the grade of meat by looking at it.

On these pages are pictures of cuts of fresh meat which are often by-passed in favor of popular steaks, chops, and roasts. Look for these bargain buys and try the recipes in this book for cooking them. You'll come up with dandy dinners—and what's more, your meat dollar will go a long way!

This beef cut is a sirloin-tip roast—a boneless triangular cut weighing 3 to 4 pounds. Makes a perfect pot roast—see recipe on page 29. Other good beef bargains: Arm or round-bone pot roast; blade-bone pot roast; boned rump pot roast; heel of round.

How to make these cuts fork tender, full of wonderful flavor? About 3 hours of cooking time—moderate heat in the oven, or simmering temperature (below boiling) on the top of the range—and cooking *covered* with a little liquid in the pan.

When you want to pull in the purse strings, take a look at beef short ribs (shown above). They are the tip ends of the elegant rib roast. Cut in 2- to 4-inch lengths, they have layers of lean meat and fat, and a bone along one side. Can't beat them for a homespun, satisfying meal. (See directions for preparing them on page 33.)

True, short ribs—and most of the other penny-wise beef cuts—require long, lazy cooking, but they pay you back in delicious flavor.

The shoulder cushion was a stand-by pork cut for generations. And it's well to renew acquaintance with this fine old-time favorite— makes the kind of savory roast that folks like to come home to, does away with meal monotony.

At the fresh-pork section of the meat case, look for boned cushion picnic shoulder—or ask for butt end of shoulder (at right). Weight varies from 3 to 8 pounds. If sold with bone in at your market, ask to have the bone removed.

Fill pocket of this pork roast with an herb-seasoned stuffing—recipe, page 38.

If you're overlooking these "different" meat cuts, you're missing out on some mighty good eating.

The smart buy pictured at right is a boneless shoulder butt—a cured and smoked pork cut sold under a number of different brand names. This is a 2½-pounder, but they vary from 1 to 6 pounds.

Slow cooking and a glaze turn a shoulder butt into company fare. See the recipe on page 50.

Lamb is usually tender. But riblets (shown at right), neck slices, stew meat, shanks, breast, and blade-bone shoulder chops take well to moist heat of braising.

For flavor accent, cook lamb in a sauce that's tangy with lemon or tomato, or both—see recipe on page 56. Or rub the uncooked meat with garlic or herbs such as rosemary, thyme, or marjoram. *Always* serve lamb piping hot. Pair it off with horseradish, capers, mint jelly or mint sauce.

No matter what season you serve lamb, it brings spring to the table. And the price of those good but not-so-fancy cuts—like the shoulder chops at right—will help put your budget in clover.

Shoulder chops are most obliging—you can broil them (see recipe on page 54), pan broil in skillet, or braise (covered) in oven or on top of range. They cook in a jiffy.

Say the word "veal" and most people think of cutlets. But there are just as tasty cuts that cost less. Take veal shoulder shown at right.

Cut up this meat for City Chicken (recipe, page 58), or in some markets you'll find the cubes of veal shoulder already strung on wood skewers. Give them a jacket of crumbs, cook tender at a slow bubble.

For your "specialty of the house," how about barbecuing breast of veal? That's the cut you see at right. If the meat is not boned and cubed, ask the meatman to do it.

Veal responds well to the gentle, moist heat of braising. Slow-cook the delicately flavored cubes of veal in an almost-sweet, tomato-y sauce. (See recipe on page 63.)

More veal "buys": shoulder steaks, rolled shoulder roast.

Canned, frozen, ready-for-the-table—take a look at these meats, too

When you shop the meat case, check the row upon row of sausage products and ready-for-the-table meats. Sausage, franks, cold cuts—they all come in dozens of different shapes, forms, and colors. They'll add special flavor treats to main dishes—don't save them just for the wiener roast and the lunch-box sandwich.

Step over to the endless variety of the frozen meat and canned meat sections. Read the labels on the packages or cans to see how easily these meats go to the table.

No reason to settle down to monotonous meals starring just 3 or 4 meats. One glance at the array of meat available . . . one look at the good ideas in this book—you'll get know-how and inspiration to serve a different meat every day of the year!

Meat is money–store it right

Leftover meat: Refrigerate in covered dish. Do not grind or chop until ready to use. Save gravy in covered jar in refrigerator, ready to season hash or meat pie.

Roasts: If not already in transparent wrapper, unwrap roast, store in meat compartment. Lay piece of clear plastic wrap or waxed paper loosely over meat. Roasts may be held 5 to 7 days.

Tips on refrigerator storage of meat

Fresh meats: Meats purchased in transparent wrapping can be stored wrapped in the meat compartment of refrigerator. Otherwise unwrap meat and place clear plastic wrap or waxed paper loosely atop.

Cured and smoked meats: Store in refrigerator in original wrapper.

Canned meats: All canned meats keep on the cupboard shelf except the large canned hams marked "Perishable. Keep refrigerated." These *must* be kept in the refrigerator.

Cooked meats: Cover and refrigerate.

Poultry: Wrap loosely in waxed paper or saran wrapping and refrigerate. To store stuffed cooked poultry: Remove stuffing, cover, and refrigerate separately.

Fish: Wrap tightly in waxed paper, saran wrapping, or aluminum foil; refrigerate.

Game: Store game birds and small animals the same as poultry; treat venison and other large animals the same as beef.

Tips on freezer storage of meat

● Package meat tightly in moisture-vaporproof wrapping or container especially made for freezer storage. A good wrap helps prevent "freezer burn," keeps meat juicy, flavorful.

● Mark each package or container with the name of the meat; the number of pieces for chops, short ribs, etc.; and the date, so you'll use the meat within the accepted storage time.

● Freeze meat at 0° or less. The faster meat freezes, the better its quality will be retained. Use meats as soon as is practical after freezing—they don't improve with age.

● For more information on foods for the freezer, turn to page 140.

Refrigerator storage time chart*

For meats held in a household refrigerator at 32° to 40°

Kind of meat	Time limit for maximum quality	Kind of meat	Time limit for maximum quality
BEEF		**LAMB**	
Large pieces (roasts, pot roasts)...........	5 to 7 days	Roasts................	5 days
Steaks..............	3 to 5 days	Chops, riblets, stew meat, shanks.........	3 days
Stew meat, ground beef, liver (sliced), heart.....	2 days	Ground lamb.........	2 days
PORK		**POULTRY**	
Large pieces (roasts, cured hams)..........	5 to 7 days	Chickens, ducklings (drawn, whole)........	2 to 3 days
Canned hams (unopened)	3 months	Chickens, etc. (cut-up)..	2 days
Bacon...............	7 days	Turkeys (drawn, whole).	4 to 5 days
Chops, spareribs.......	3 days		
Pork sausage..........	2 days	**COOKED MEATS**	
Liver (sliced)..........	2 days	Home-cooked meats....	2 days
		Cooked poultry........	2 days
VEAL		Hams, picnics.........	7 days
		Frankfurters..........	4 to 5 days
Roasts...............	5 to 7 days	Luncheon meats (sliced)	3 to 4 days
Chops...............	4 days	Unsliced loaves, bologna	4 to 6 days
Stew meat...........	3 days	Liver sausage (sliced)...	2 to 3 days
Ground veal, liver (sliced)...............	2 days	Liver sausage (unsliced).	4 to 6 days
		Sweetbreads..........	2 days
		Dry-type sausage (uncut)	2 to 3 weeks

*Any chart can be only a guide. So many factors can vary: quality and age of the meat when purchased, preparation, handling, conditions in and efficiency of home refrigerator. (In some refrigerators, flowing cold air increases the storage life of fresh meat.) Meats do not improve with storage—use while fresh to get benefit of the quality you paid for.

Freezer storage time chart**

For meats stored in a household freezer at 0° or lower.

Beef.................	6 to 8 months	Fresh pork sausage, bologna, sliced bacon, frankfurters..........	Do not freeze
Fresh pork and veal....	3 to 4 months		
Lamb................	6 to 7 months		
Ground meat, variety meats...............	3 to 4 months	Chicken (ready to cook).	6 to 7 months
		Turkey (ready to cook).	6 to 8 months
		Cooked meat and chicken	2 to 3 months
Smoked hams, picnic, slab bacon...........	2 months	Fish and sea food......	3 to 6 months

**This chart gives storage times for properly wrapped meats of good quality, held not more than 10 days as fresh meat before freezing. Times given are limit for top quality.

1 Roasting

2 Broiling

3 Pan-broiling

4 Pan-frying

Meat cookery

Follow these rules for juicy, fork-tender meat

Whatever meat you choose, learn the best method for cooking it—the method that makes it tender and moist. On these pages are some general principles and basic methods for cooking meat. Turn the page to see the method to use for cooking the cut of meat you bought. You'll find more specific information in the recipes. Don't forget to read the labels on all packaged and canned meats—then follow the directions.

Cooking meat really involves two methods—cooking with dry heat or moist heat, depending on whether liquid is used. Each of these basic methods has several variations.

Dry heat methods	Moist heat methods
Roasting	Braising
Broiling	Cooking in water
Pan-broiling	Stewing
Pan-frying	Pressure cooking
Rotisserie cooking	

Beef may be served rare, medium, or well-done—depending on how your family likes it. Serve lamb medium or well-done. Veal is best served well-done. Pork should always be cooked to the well-done stage. See recipes for meat thermometer readings.

1 Roasting

Sprinkle meat with salt and pepper, if desired. Insert meat thermometer so that bulb reaches center of the largest muscle. Bulb should not rest in fat or on bone.

Place meat, fat side up, on a rack in open pan. (A rack need not be used for standing rib roast—bones make rack.) Meat will brown as it roasts. Do not cover. Do not add water and do not baste. Roast in slow oven (325°) till done. See recipes for roasting times and thermometer readings.

2 Broiling

Steaks and chops should be cut at least 1 inch thick for broiling; slices of ham should be at least ½ inch thick.

Preheat broiler, if desired. Place meat on rack of broiling pan. The top surface of 1-inch steaks or chops should be 2 to 3 inches from the heat; 2-inch cuts, 3 to 5 inches from heat. Reduce temperature if distance must be less. Broil top side till nicely browned. Season with salt and pepper. Turn and broil second side till browned and meat is done. (One turning is all that's necessary.)

5 Braising

6 Cooking in water

7 Stewing

8 Rotisserie

Season second side and serve at once. Broiling time depends on thickness of meat and degree of doneness desired. (See broiling recipes and timetables.) To check for doneness of *beef*, cut a slit in the meat and note the color inside: Rare beef will be red; medium—pink; well-done—gray.

3 Pan-broiling

Preheat a heavy skillet. Rub the skillet with some meat fat to prevent sticking. Brown meat on both sides. Season.

Reduce temperature and finish cooking. Do not cover. Do not add water. Pour off fat as it accumulates in the pan. Turn occasionally to cook meat evenly.

4 Pan-frying

Brown meat quickly in small amount of fat. Season with salt and pepper. Reduce heat and cook, uncovered, until meat is done.

This method is often used for round steak, liver, veal steaks and chops, and other meats low in natural fat.

5 Braising

Roll or dip meat in flour, if desired. Brown slowly on all sides in hot fat. Season with salt and pepper; add herbs and spices, if desired. Add a very small amount of liquid, if necessary to prevent sticking. (Tomato juice or bouillon may be used to add more flavor.) Cover pan with tight-fitting lid—this holds in the steam and makes the meat tender. Finish cooking at simmering on range top or in slow to moderate oven (325°-350°).

6 Cooking in water

Cover meat with water or other liquid. Add seasonings (unless meat is already seasoned —corned beef, smoked pork butt). Cover and simmer, don't boil, till meat is fork-tender. See recipes for approximate times.

If meat is to be served cold or used later, cool meat and stock to room temperature. Then refrigerate meat in the stock.

7 Stewing

Cut meat in uniform pieces, usually 1- to 2-inch cubes. Roll or dip in flour, if desired. Brown slowly on all sides in a small amount of hot fat. Season with salt and pepper; add herbs and spices, if desired. Add hot water to just cover meat. Cover pan with tight-fitting lid. Cook at simmering temperature (185°) until meat is tender. It's important to keep heat *low*—never boil meat.

About an hour before meat is done, add vegetables. (See recipes for good vegetable combinations and cooking times.) Thicken the hot liquid for gravy.

8 Rotisserie cooking

Follow general directions for roasting or broiling. For specific meat cuts, use directions that come with the appliance.

Pressure cooking

Follow general directions for braising, stewing, or cooking in water. For specific cuts, follow the directions that come with the pressure pan. Also, see recipes.

Beef cuts and how to cook them

Standing rib
Roast

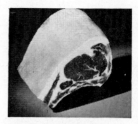

Rolled rib
Roast

Sirloin steak
Broil, pan-broil, pan-fry

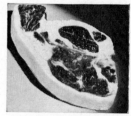

Pinbone sirloin steak
Broil, pan-broil, pan-fry

Porterhouse steak
Broil, pan-broil, pan-fry

T-bone steak
Broil, pan-broil, pan-fry

Club steak
Broil, pan-broil, pan-fry

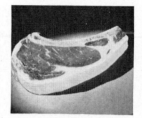

Rib steak
Broil, pan-broil, pan-fry

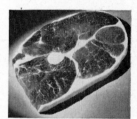

Round steak (*full cut*)
Braise

Top round steak
Broil, pan-broil, pan-fry, braise

Bottom round steak
Braise

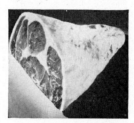

Heel of round
Braise, cook in liquid

Rolled rump
Braise, roast

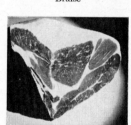

Standing rump
Braise, roast

Blade pot roast (*chuck*)
Braise

Boneless chuck
Braise

English cut (*chuck*)
Braise

Arm pot roast (*chuck*)
Braise

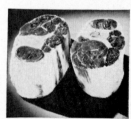

Shank cross cuts
Cook in liquid, braise

Short ribs
Braise, cook in liquid

Flank steak
Braise

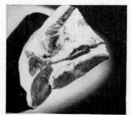

Brisket (*bone in*)
Braise, cook in liquid

Corned beef (*brisket*)
Cook in liquid

Plate beef
Braise, cook in liquid

Pork cuts and how to cook them

Loin roast (*center cut*)
Roast

Sirloin roast
Roast

Boneless sirloin roast
Roast

Blade loin roast
Roast

Crown roast
Roast

Fresh picnic shoulder
Roast

Arm roast (*shoulder*)
Roast

Arm steak (*shoulder*)
Braise, pan-fry

Boston butt (*shoulder*)
Roast

Tenderloin
Roast, braise, pan-fry

Loin chops
Braise, pan-fry

Rib chops
Braise, pan-fry

Blade steak (*shoulder*)
Braise, pan-fry

Spareribs
Roast (bake), braise,
cook in liquid

Half ham (*shank end*)
Roast (bake), cook in liquid

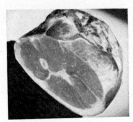

Half ham (*butt end*)
Roast (bake), cook in liquid

Center ham slice
Broil, pan-broil, pan-fry

Smoked picnic
shoulder
Roast, cook in liquid

Smoked shoulder butt
Roast, cook in liquid, broil,
pan-broil, pan-fry

Canadian-style bacon
Roast, broil, pan-broil, pan-fry

Sliced bacon
Broil, bake, pan-broil,
pan-fry

Salt pork (*side*)
Cook in liquid, pan-broil,
pan-fry

Jowl bacon square
Cook in liquid, broil,
pan-broil, pan-fry

Hocks
Braise, cook in liquid

Lamb cuts and how to cook them

American leg
Roast

Frenched leg
Roast

Boneless sirloin roast
Roast

Rolled loin
Roast

Loin roast
Roast

Rib roast (*rack*)
Roast

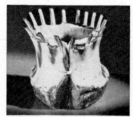

Crown roast
Roast

Square-cut shoulder
Roast

Cushion shoulder
Roast

Rolled shoulder
Roast, braise

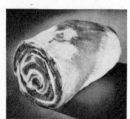

Rolled breast
Braise, roast

Breast
Braise, roast

Sirloin chops
Broil, pan-broil, pan-fry

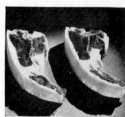

Loin chops
Broil, pan-broil, pan-fry

English chops
Broil, pan-broil, pan-fry

Rib chops
Broil, pan-broil, pan-fry

Frenched chops (*rib*)
Broil, pan-broil, pan-fry

Shoulder chops
Broil, pan-broil, pan-fry, braise

Saratoga chops (*shoulder*)
Broil, pan-broil, pan-fry, braise

Patties
Broil, pan-broil, pan-fry

Ground lamb
Roast (bake)

Riblets (*breast*)
Braise, cook in liquid

Shanks
Braise, cook in liquid

Neck slices
Braise, cook in liquid

Veal cuts and how to cook them

Rib roast
Roast

Sirloin roast
Roast, braise

Loin roast
Roast, braise

Shank half of leg
Roast, braise

Standing rump
Roast, braise

Rolled rump roast
Roast, braise

Center cut of leg
Roast, braise

Heel of round
Braise, cook in liquid

Blade roast (*shoulder*)
Roast, braise

Arm roast (*shoulder*)
Roast, braise

Rolled shoulder
Roast, braise

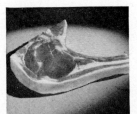

Rib chop
Braise, pan-fry

Sirloin steak
Braise, pan-fry

Loin chop
Braise, pan-fry

Kidney chop
Braise, pan-fry

Round steak (*cutlet*)
Braise, pan-fry

Mock chicken legs
Braise, pan-fry

City chicken
Braise, pan-fry

Arm steak (*shoulder*)
Braise, pan-fry

Blade steak (*shoulder*)
Braise, pan-fry

Breast
Roast, braise, cook in liquid

Riblets (*breast*)
Braise, cook in liquid

Fore shank
Braise, cook in liquid

Boneless stew
Braise, cook in liquid

Beef—
cook to a T, carve to perfection!

Standing Rib Roast of Beef

Select a 3- or 4-rib standing rib roast of beef. Place fat side up in roasting pan; season with salt and pepper. Insert meat thermometer so tip reaches center of thickest muscle. Place in slow oven (325°). Do not add water; do not cover.

Roast to desired degree of doneness. Allow 20 to 22 minutes *per pound* for rare roast, 24 to 27 minutes *per pound* for medium, and 29 to 32 minutes *per pound* for well-done roast. Meat thermometer will read 140° for rare, 160° for medium, 170° for well-done beef. Count on 2 or 3 servings per pound of meat. (Roast Potatoes, page 22.)

Dad, here are tips to make you a star performer when it comes to carving. Be sure the knife is sharp. A 9-inch blade is a good length for carving roasts. Take a look at the roast in the kitchen to get acquainted before dinnertime.

Sit or stand, as you choose, while carving at the table. Always carve across the grain of the meat—the fibers will be shorter, more easily eaten. For smooth slices, cut with a firm motion. Avoid sawing back and forth, or changing the angle of the knife. Carve slices for firsts for everyone before serving any of the plates. Wait to carve the seconds till folks are ready.

Hints for Mother, Dad's assistant . . . make it easy for him! Ask the meat dealer to separate the backbone from the ribs; remove it in the kitchen after roasting. Let the roast stand for about 15 minutes to firm before carving. Choose a platter about 2 inches larger all around than the roast. Keep garnishes simple, or they'll complicate Dad's job. Heat the platter and plates. If there won't be room on the platter for the slices as they're cut, put small heated platter alongside.

For *beef au jus*, skim fat from pan drippings of beef roast—serve the natural meat juices without thickening. Or, make Perfect Gravy—recipe, page 93.

It's easy to carve a standing rib roast of beef—here's how

Cut surface is up, backbone is removed from ribs, rib side is at the left. Insert fork between top ribs. Cut from outside edge across to the rib.

To loosen the slice, cut along the bone with the tip of the carving knife at a vertical angle. You'll need a good sharp knife to do the job easily.

Lift the slice with the carving knife, steadying it with the fork. Place to one side of the platter or on extra plate alongside. Slice ⅜-inch-thick slices.

**Standing Rib Roast of Beef—
a first choice of everybody!**

What main dish could be easier? No measuring, no mixing! Serve tender, juicy roast with Roast Potatoes (recipe on next page), and buttered peas and carrots.

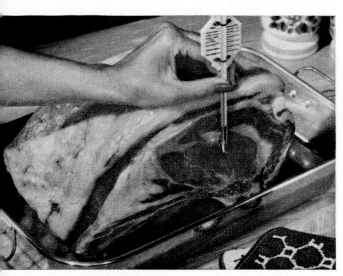

The tip of meat thermometer goes in the center of the roast, so measure distance as shown above. With metal skewer make hole for thermometer in thickest part. Bulb must not touch bone or fat.

Roast uncovered in slow oven (325°). The meat thermometer will read 140° for rare, 160° for medium, and 170° for well done. See the recipe (preceding page) for approximate roasting times.

Place rolled rib roast fat side up on rack in shallow roasting pan. Roast at constant low temperature (325°).

Use a meat thermometer—that's the only sure way to tell when roast is done to your liking. Insert so tip of thermometer is in center of roast.

(Don't add water, don't cover.) Roast till meat thermometer says "when." Some ranges have roast-meters—doneness of meat shows on control panel.

Rolled Rib Roast of Beef

Select boned and rolled rib roast. Place fat side up on rack in shallow roasting pan; season with salt and pepper. Insert meat thermometer into center of roast. Do not add water. Roast uncovered in slow oven (325°) to desired doneness. Allow 30 to 32 minutes *per pound* for rare; 34 to 37 minutes *per pound* for medium; and 39 to 42 minutes *per pound* for well-done. Meat thermometer will read 140° for rare; 160° for medium; and 170° for well-done.

Let roast stand 15 minutes to firm before carving. Three to 4 servings per pound. See finished roast on page 5.

Roast Potatoes

Pare medium potatoes; cook in boiling, salted water 15 minutes; drain.

About 45 minutes before roast is done (325°), place hot potatoes in meat drippings around roast, turning potatoes to coat. Roast till potatoes are done, turning occasionally. Season with salt; serve hot.

Rump Roast

A rump roast of *top-quality* beef may be roasted by the same method used for standing rib roast; if the roast is rolled, follow method for rolled rib roast. Cook rump roasts to medium- or well-done stage. Three to 4 servings per pound.

More ways to cook rump roast—page 28.

Rib-eye Roast of Beef

The king of roasts! See it on the cover. This beef cut may be new in some markets, so if you don't see it, ask your meatman.

Roast as you would a rolled rib roast, but allow about 30 minutes per pound for medium. Use meat thermometer to be sure it's done the way you like it.

Roast Beef Tenderloin

Remove fat surface from whole beef tenderloin (4 to 6 pounds). Place on rack in open pan. Tuck under small ends; top ends with some of the fat, or foil.

Brush meat with salad oil. Cut gashes; insert cut garlic cloves. Roast in very hot oven (450°) 45 to 60 minutes or till meat thermometer registers 140°. Remove garlic.

Stuffed Beef Tenderloin

1 3-pound beef tenderloin
½ small onion, chopped
1 3-ounce can (⅔ cup) mushrooms
1½ cups soft bread crumbs
½ cup diced celery

Have meatman split and flatten tenderloin. Lightly brown onion, mushrooms in ¼ cup butter. Add crumbs, celery, *and enough hot water to moisten*. Season with salt and pepper. Spread stuffing over half the meat.

Fold second half over; fasten edges. Season; top with 4 bacon slices. Roast at 350° about 1 hour. Makes 6 to 8 servings.

Mighty special eating—steak

Serve it sizzling . . . broiled just the way you like it!

Kitchen duty is minimum—follow these easy steps

Broiled Steak

Select a porterhouse, T-bone, club, sirloin, or tenderloin (filet mignon) steak cut 1 to 2 inches thick. Slash the fatty edge of the steak—don't cut into meat.

Place steak on broiler rack so that top surface is 3 to 5 inches from the heat (for well-done, 5 inches; for rare to medium, 3 to 5 inches). If the distance must be less, reduce the temperature accordingly.

Broil on one side; season with salt and pepper. Turn, broil on other side. Season and serve immediately on heated platter.

For 1-inch steak, allow total of 15 to 20 minutes; for 1½-inch steak, 20 to 25 minutes; for 2-inch steak, 30 to 35 minutes.

To test for doneness, cut a slit in the meat and note the color inside: red—rare; pink—medium; gray—well-done.

Variations of Broiled Steak

Cross-cut Steak: Have porterhouse or sirloin steak cut 2 inches thick. Slash the fat edge. Broil 5 to 7 inches from heat. For medium steak, allow about 55 minutes total broiling time. To serve, slice in 1-inch strips crosswise. See picture on page 2.

Planked Steak: Broil meat on broiler rack. When nearly done, place meat on wooden plank. With pastry tube, pipe border of mashed potatoes around meat; brown in hot oven. Add other cooked vegetables.

Tendered Steak: Choose less costly steak—round, rump, or chuck. Sprinkle meat with nonseasoned meat tenderizer according to package directions. Broil meat to desired doneness. Meat tenderizer cuts cooking time, so be careful not to overcook the steak you choose.

Zesty hot-off-the-grill specials—Steaks Bonaparte, glazed onions

Trim fat from four ½-inch club steaks. Melt two tablespoons garlic butter on hot sandwich grill; dip steaks. Cook about 5 minutes per side.

Push steaks aside. Mix a tablespoon each lemon juice and Worcestershire on grill; swish steaks through. Serve on toasted garlic French bread.

Serve steak all kinds of ways

Pan-broiled Steak

Select same steaks as for broiling, cut ½ to ¾ inch thick. Place in preheated heavy frying pan. Do not use fat in pan. Brown on each side. Reduce heat; cook to desired degree of doneness, pouring off fat as it accumulates. Turn occasionally to cook uniformly. Total cooking time for rare steak is about 12 minutes; for medium- or well-done steak, 18 to 24 minutes. Season and serve.

Chicken-fried Round Steak

1½ to 2 pounds round steak,
　½ inch thick
2 beaten eggs
2 tablespoons milk
1 cup fine cracker crumbs
¼ cup fat
Salt and pepper

Pound steak thoroughly, or ask meatman to do it. Cut steak into serving pieces.

Mix eggs and milk. Dip meat into egg mixture, then into cracker crumbs. Handle carefully so all the coating stays on.

Brown on both sides in hot fat. Season. Cover tightly and cook over very low heat 45 to 60 minutes. Makes 6 servings.

Home-style Steak

½ cup enriched flour
2 tablespoons dry mustard
1 teaspoon salt
Dash pepper
2 pounds round steak, 1 inch thick
Fat
1 can condensed tomato soup
½ cup chopped onion
2 tablespoons Worcestershire sauce

Combine flour, mustard, salt, and pepper; pound into steak with meat pounder. Brown slowly in a little hot fat; drain off excess fat. Combine tomato soup, onion, and Worcestershire sauce; pour over meat. Bake uncovered in slow oven (325°) 1½ hours or till tender. Makes 6 servings.

Minute Steaks

Minute steaks are thin cuts from the round, that have been scored by a special machine to cut connective tissue. Rub hot skillet with a little fat. Cook steaks quickly, usually 1 or 2 minutes on each side. Season with salt and pepper. Serve with Hashed Browns and fried onion rings, if desired.

Hashed Browns: Chill cooked-in-jacket potatoes; peel, shred. Add grated onion, salt, and pepper. Melt fat in skillet to cover bottom well. Pat potatoes into pan, leaving *½-inch space around edge.* Brown 10 to 12 minutes; peek. When crusty and hot, place platter over pan; invert.

Skillet Pizza Steak

Brown six ¼-pound minute steaks in hot olive or salad oil. Add 1 clove garlic, minced, two 8-ounce cans (2 cups) seasoned tomato sauce, ¾ cup water, 1 teaspoon oregano, ½ teaspoon basil, and dash pepper. Simmer uncovered, turning steaks occasionally, till meat is tender (45 to 60 minutes).

Top each steak with thin slice Mozzarella cheese. Skim off any excess fat. Serves 6.

Beef Kabobs

Cut beef (round or sirloin) in 1- to 1½-inch cubes. (Two pounds beef cubes make about 6 servings.) If you choose round, pierce cubes with fork; sprinkle with meat tenderizer, following label directions. Let meat stand in Beef Marinade* 2 hours.

On long skewers, alternate whole fresh mushrooms, beef cubes, and ½-inch slices of cucumber. Save room for tomatoes.

Place skewers 4 to 5 inches from the heat. Broil about 25 minutes, turning frequently and basting often with Beef Marinade.

About the last 5 minutes of cooking, add small tomatoes to the ends of skewers.

Beef Marinade: Combine ½ cup salad oil, ¼ cup vinegar, ¼ cup chopped onion, 1 teaspoon salt, 2 teaspoons Worcestershire sauce.

Minute Steaks and Hashed Browns—mighty good! The steaks are juicy, still a little pink inside. Potatoes boast a crisp crust that's browned to a turn. Serve *hot* on a *hot* platter, with panned onion slices, a big tossed salad.

Oven Round-steak Dinner

2 pounds round steak, 1 inch thick,
   cut into serving pieces
6 medium onions, sliced
¼ cup fat
3 large potatoes, halved
1 bay leaf
1 can condensed tomato soup
1 1-pound can (2 cups) French-cut
   green beans, drained

Season meat with 2 teaspoons salt and dash pepper. Roll in flour. Cook onions in hot fat till tender but not brown; remove onions and brown meat slowly on both sides. Place meat in 3-quart casserole; add onions, potatoes, and bay leaf; pour soup over.

Cover; bake at 350° 1 hour and 45 minutes or till meat is tender. Add beans; cook 10 to 15 minutes more. Makes 6 to 8 servings.

Swiss Steak in Foil

1 cup catsup
¼ cup enriched flour
2 pounds round steak, 1 inch thick
1 large onion, sliced
2 tablespoons lemon juice, or 1 lemon,
   thinly sliced (optional)

Tear off 5-foot length of household-weight aluminum foil; fold double. Combine catsup and flour; spoon *half* of mixture in center of foil. Place steak atop; season with salt and pepper. Cover meat with onion slices and remaining catsup mixture. Sprinkle with lemon juice or top with lemon slices. Fold foil over and seal edges securely.

Place in shallow baking pan. Bake in very hot oven (450°) for 1½ hours or till meat is tender. Remove foil; cut steak in pieces. Makes 5 or 6 servings.

Home-style steak—thrifty, too

These tender, full-of-flavor steaks give a T-bone real competition! Here's what to serve with them.

Swiss Steak: Baked potatoes, garlic bread, coleslaw, canned peaches, brownies.

Steak 'n Potato Supper: Buttered whole carrots, Waldorf salad, gingerbread.

Minute-steak Rolls: Green beans with almonds, Italian salad, pickled peppers, and apple pie with cheese.

Minute-steak Rolls

6 minute steaks
1 3-ounce can (⅔ cup) broiled chopped mushrooms
½ cup snipped parsley
½ cup chopped onion
½ cup shredded or grated Parmesan cheese
1 10½-ounce can condensed beef broth
2 tablespoons cornstarch

Pound steaks if thick. Drain mushrooms, reserving liquid. Sprinkle chopped mushrooms, parsley, onion, and cheese over steaks; season lightly with salt and pepper. Starting at narrow end, tightly roll up each steak; fasten with toothpicks. Brown steak rolls *slowly* in 2 tablespoons hot fat in skillet. Add *half* of the beef broth.

Cover; simmer 30 to 45 minutes or till tender. Remove steaks to hot platter. Combine cornstarch, reserved mushroom liquid, and remaining broth; stir into skillet. Cook, stirring constantly, till thick. Spoon over meat rolls; sprinkle with additional Parmesan cheese. Garnish with tomato wedges and celery leaves. Serves 6.

← *In the electric skillet: Steak 'n Potato Supper; above: Swiss Steak; arranged on platter: Flavorful Minute-steak Rolls.*

Swiss Steak

Pizza sauce is the new seasoning trick—

⅓ cup enriched flour
2 teaspoons salt
¼ teaspoon pepper
2 pounds round or chuck steak, 1 inch thick
3 tablespoons fat

· · ·

1 8-ounce can (1 cup) seasoned tomato sauce
2 5½-ounce cans (1⅓ cups) pizza sauce
1 medium onion, sliced

Combine flour, salt, and pepper; pound into steak. Brown *slowly* on both sides in hot fat. Pour tomato sauce and pizza sauce over meat. Top with onion slices. Simmer uncovered 10 minutes.

Cover and bake in oven-going skillet or large casserole in moderate oven (350°) 1 hour or a little longer, until the steak is fork-tender. Makes 6 servings.

Steak 'n Potato Supper

1½ pounds round steak, ½ inch thick
¼ cup enriched flour
2 teaspoons salt
¼ teaspoon pepper
2 tablespoons fat
1 can condensed beef broth

· · ·

4 medium potatoes, pared and cut in ¼-inch slices
2 medium onions, thinly sliced

Cut steak in serving-size pieces. Combine flour, salt, and pepper; coat the meat with flour mixture. In skillet, brown meat *slowly* in hot fat—this should take 20 to 30 minutes. Add broth. Cover tightly and simmer (don't boil) 30 minutes or till almost tender. Add a little water if needed. (When using electric skillet, follow manufacturer's directions for correct settings for browning, simmering.)

Place potato and onion slices over meat. Season vegetables with salt and pepper. Cover tightly; cook *slowly* about 35 minutes longer or till potatoes are done. Snip parsley atop. Makes 6 servings.

Good eating—pot roast

Beef Pot Roast

Select a 3- to 4-pound chuck or rump pot roast. Trim excess fat from roast; heat fat in large skillet or Dutch oven.

Roll pot roast in flour; brown on all sides in hot fat. Season with salt and pepper.

Add ½ cup water. Cover tightly and cook slowly 2½ to 3 hours or till tender. Add more water if needed to prevent sticking.

If desired, add small whole onions and carrots the last 45 minutes of cooking.

Thicken liquid for Pot-roast Gravy, if desired. Makes 6 to 8 servings.

Variations of Beef Pot Roast

1. Cut ½-inch slits in pot roast and insert ¼ pound salt pork cut in strips.

Add one 1-pound can (2 cups) tomatoes, 3 medium onions (sliced), salt, pepper, ½ teaspoon cloves, ½ teaspoon marjoram, 4 whole black peppers, and ⅓ cup vinegar.

2. Add chopped onion, chopped celery, sliced carrots, and potatoes the last 45 minutes of cooking.

Fifteen minutes before serving, pour ½ cup chili sauce, ¼ cup hot water, and 1 teaspoon Worcestershire sauce over meat.

3. Use tomato juice instead of water for the cooking liquid. Or you might like condensed beef broth from a can.

4. Slice 2 small onions over meat after browning. Add 2 bay leaves and 5 whole cloves. Use ¼ cup vinegar and ¼ cup water as the cooking liquid.

5. Cook 2 cups cranberries with 1 cup water until skins pop. Pour over meat after browning. Baste meat with cranberries several times during cooking.

6. After browning, season pot roast with salt, pepper, and 1 tablespoon dill seed. Slice 2 medium onions; place slices atop meat. Cook as directed above. (Potato halves and carrots may be added the last hour.) Serve with Sour Cream Gravy.

Sauerbraten

6 pounds beef rump
5 cups vinegar
5 cups water
3 onions, sliced
1 lemon, sliced
12 whole cloves
6 bay leaves
6 whole black peppers
3 tablespoons salt

Place meat in large bowl; add other ingredients. Let stand 36 hours* in refrigerator; turn occasionally.

Remove meat; brown in hot fat. Add 1 cup vinegar mixture; cover; cook slowly 2 hours or till tender; add water if necessary. Makes 8 to 10 servings.

*For mild flavor, soak meat only 24 hours.

Pot-roast Gravy

Skim most of fat from meat stock. For 1½ to 2 cups stock, use these proportions: Put ½ cup cold water into a shaker, then add ¼ cup enriched flour; shake to mix. (Or place flour in small bowl. Stir in a little of the water to make smooth paste; then stir in remaining water.)

Remove stock from heat and slowly stir in flour mixture. Return to heat and cook, stirring constantly, till gravy is bubbling all over. Now add kitchen bouquet, if desired. Season to taste with salt and pepper. Continue cooking about 5 minutes more, stirring occasionally.

Sour Cream Gravy: For 1½ to 2 cups meat stock, blend 1 cup dairy sour cream and 3 tablespoons enriched flour. Remove stock from heat and slowly stir in sour-cream mixture. Cook, stirring constantly, just until gravy thickens.

Braised Sirloin-tip Roast with vegetables, gravy

All the homespun flavors mingle in this meal-in-one special. If you wish, cook it slowly in covered Dutch oven, top of range—instead of in oven. Add water, if needed.

Braised Sirloin-tip Roast

3 to 4 pounds sirloin-tip roast
Enriched flour
1 medium onion, sliced
2 bay leaves
1 clove garlic, minced
½ cup hot water
8 small onions, peeled
8 medium carrots, pared
8 small potatoes, pared

Sprinkle meat lightly with flour and rub in. Brown slowly on all sides in a little hot fat in Dutch oven. Season with 2 teaspoons salt and ¼ teaspoon pepper. Add sliced onion, bay leaves, garlic, and water. Cover and cook in moderate oven (350°) about 1½ hours or till almost tender.

Add vegetables; sprinkle with 1½ teaspoons salt. Cover and cook 1 hour or till meat and vegetables are done. Thicken liquid for Pot-roast Gravy (recipe on preceding page). Makes 6 to 8 servings.

Fruited Pot Roast

12 dried prunes
12 dried apricots
3½ to 4 pounds arm pot roast
1½ cups sliced onions
1 cup apple cider
2 tablespoons sugar
¼ teaspoon cinnamon
¼ teaspoon ginger
3 whole cloves

Cover prunes and apricots with water; soak several hours. Heat fat from meat in heavy skillet or Dutch oven. Dip meat in flour; brown well on all sides in hot fat. Season with 2 teaspoons salt and ¼ teaspoon pepper. Add onions. Combine cider, sugar, and spices; pour half over meat. Cover and simmer 1 hour; add remaining liquid and cook 1 to 1½ hours longer, or till meat is tender.

Drain prunes and apricots; place on roast for last 30 minutes of cooking. Thicken liquid for gravy. Makes 6 to 8 servings.

A favorite – old-time
beef stew

Husky cubes of meat and whole, just-tender vegetables, all expertly seasoned—here's a stew folks will rave about! Long, slow cooking is the secret for its perfect flavor.

Old-time Beef Stew

It's a cook's masterpiece!—

2 pounds beef chuck, cut in 1½-inch cube.
2 tablespoons fat
4 cups boiling water
1 tablespoon lemon juice (optional)
1 teaspoon Worcestershire sauce
1 clove garlic
1 medium onion, sliced
1 to 2 bay leaves
1 tablespoon salt
1 teaspoon sugar
½ teaspoon pepper
½ teaspoon paprika
Dash allspice or cloves
6 carrots
1 pound (18 to 24) small white onions

BETTER HOMES AND GARDENS
ECONOMY RECIPE

Thoroughly brown the meat on all sides in hot fat; add water, lemon juice, Worcestershire sauce, garlic, sliced onion, bay leaves, and seasonings. Cover; simmer 2 hours, stirring occasionally to keep from sticking. Remove bay leaves and garlic.

Add carrots and onions. (Cubed potatoes may be added, too.) Cover and cook 30 minutes more, or till vegetables are done. Remove meat and vegetables. Thicken liquid for gravy, if desired (recipe, next page). Makes 6 to 8 servings.

Follow the pictures for a hearty beef stew you'll be proud of. Ladle ou

1 In Dutch oven or deep heavy kettle, brown meat cubes *slowly* in a little hot fat. Don't hurry this step—it takes about 20 minutes to develop best color and flavor. Turn meat often for even browning on all sides.

2 When meat's well browned, pour in the boiling water. Lower heat and shift meat with fork to make sure cubes aren't sticking to pan. Next in go seasonings. Cover; simmer till tender—2 hours. *Don't boil.* Stir occasionally.

Gravy for Beef Stew

Skim most of fat from stew liquid. For 3 cups liquid, put ½ cup cold water in shaker or screw-top jar; add ¼ cup enriched flour. Shake flour with water to mix.

Add flour mixture slowly to meat stock, stirring constantly till gravy bubbles all over. Cook about 5 minutes more, stirring often. Pour over meat and vegetables.

Speedy Vegetable-Beef Stew

2 pounds beef chuck, cut in
   1-inch cubes
2 tablespoons fat
Salt and pepper
¾ teaspoon paprika
¼ teaspoon basil leaves
1 cup onion slices
1 cup celery slices
6 whole medium carrots
6 whole medium potatoes
1 12-ounce can (1½ cups) vegetable-
   juice cocktail

Brown meat slowly in hot fat in pressure pan (about 15 minutes). Add seasonings, vegetables, and juice. Cook at 10 or 15 pounds pressure 10 to 12 minutes. Cool pan normally 5 minutes; then reduce pressure under cold running water. Thicken stew, if desired. Makes 4 to 6 servings.

generous bowlfuls

3 Lift out bay leaves and garlic. Add vegetables. (If carrots are large, halve or quarter for faster cooking.) Simmer till vegetables are just tender. This takes about 30 minutes.

Oven Beef Stew

Combine 2 tablespoons enriched flour, 1½ teaspoons salt, and dash pepper; dip 1½ pounds 1½-inch cubes beef chuck in mixture. Brown in 2 tablespoons hot fat (reserve drippings). In 2-quart casserole place meat, 5 to 6 carrots, sliced, and 10 peeled small white onions.

Combine meat drippings with one 6-ounce can (⅔ cup) tomato paste, 1 clove garlic, minced, 1 bay leaf, dash thyme, 1 teaspoon monosodium glutamate, 1½ cups water, 1 tablespoon vinegar; bring to boiling. Pour over meat. Cover; bake in moderate oven (350°) 45 minutes. Add one 10-ounce package frozen peas; cover and bake 45 minutes more or till meat and vegetables are tender. Makes 4 to 6 servings.

Vegetable Soup

3- to 4-pound beef soup bone
1 small onion, quartered
2 cups fresh or canned tomatoes
6 sprigs parsley
2 cups chopped cabbage
¼ cup rice or barley
5 or 6 carrots, sliced
2 cups cut green beans
1 cup diced potato
½ cup chopped celery

Cut half the meat from bone and brown in a little hot fat.

Add remaining meat and bone to *2 quarts cold water.* Add browned meat, onion, and *1 teaspoon salt;* cook slowly 2 hours.

Add remaining ingredients. Cook 1 hour longer. Makes 8 to 10 servings.

Beef Stroganoff

Have 1 pound trimmed beef tenderloin sliced ¼ inch thick. Cut into strips, ¼ inch wide. Brown quickly in ¼ cup butter or margarine in skillet. Push meat to one side; add 6 ounces mushrooms, sliced (about 2 cups), and ½ cup chopped onion. Cook till tender, but not brown.

Add 1 can condensed beef broth; heat just to boiling. Blend 1 cup dairy sour cream with 2½ tablespoons enriched flour; stir into broth. Cook, stirring constantly, till thickened (sauce will be thin). Add salt and pepper to taste. Serve over hot rice or buttered noodles. Makes 4 or 5 servings.

Short-rib Stew with Parsley Dumplings. Ladle out generous helpings and be ready with seconds.

Short-rib Stew with Parsley Dumplings

Cut 2 pounds short ribs in serving pieces. Combine ¼ cup enriched flour, 1 tablespoon salt, ¼ teaspoon pepper; roll ribs in mixture. Brown in 2 tablespoons hot fat.

Combine two 1-pound cans (4 cups) tomatoes; 2 cloves garlic, minced; 1 tablespoon Worcestershire sauce. Pour over ribs. Cover; simmer 1½ hours. Add 5 carrots, sliced; 2 medium onions, sliced; 1 medium potato, diced. Simmer 45 minutes, or till meat, vegetables are tender. Skim off fat.

Season stew to taste. Drop Parsley Dumpling mixture from tablespoon atop bubbling stew. Cover tightly; bring to boiling. Reduce heat (don't lift cover) and simmer 15 minutes longer. Makes 4 or 5 servings.

Parsley Dumplings: Sift together 1 cup sifted enriched flour, 2 teaspoons baking powder, ½ teaspoon salt. Add ¼ cup chopped parsley. Combine ½ cup milk and 2 tablespoons salad oil; add to dry ingredients, stirring just till flour is dampened.

Ahwahnee Tenderloin Tips

2 tablespoons butter
1 tablespoon enriched flour
1 cup beef bouillon
1 bay leaf
3 whole cloves
2 pounds tenderloin tips, cut in thin bias strips
2 tablespoons salad oil
1 medium green pepper, cut in thin strips
½ pound fresh mushrooms, sliced
2 tablespoons butter
¼ cup lemon juice

Melt 2 tablespoons butter; blend in flour; gradually stir in bouillon. Add bay leaf and cloves; heat, stirring constantly, to boiling. Simmer 2 minutes; remove spices. Brown meat in hot oil; season with salt and pepper. Add green pepper; cook till tender.

Cook mushrooms just till tender in 2 tablespoons butter; add bouillon mixture, lemon juice, tenderloin tips. Heat to boiling; season. Trim with pimiento strips, if desired. Makes 4 to 6 servings.

Hearty short ribs–a bargain

Braised Short Ribs with Onion Gravy

3 pounds beef short ribs
Enriched flour
Salt and pepper
½ cup hot water

• • •

1 recipe traditional Onion Gravy or
Easy Onion Gravy

Trim excess fat from ribs; heat fat in Dutch oven. Roll short ribs in flour; slowly brown on all sides in the hot fat. When meat is thoroughly browned, spoon off fat. Sprinkle meat with 1 teaspoon salt and dash pepper; add water. Cover and simmer* till tender, about 2 hours. Add more water if needed during cooking. (If you use an electric saucepan, brown ribs at 400°, then reduce temperature to 200° for simmering.)

Lift meat from the stock to warm platter; keep meat hot while you make Onion Gravy. Makes about 4 servings.

*Or cover and cook in slow to moderate oven (325° to 350°) 2 hours or till tender.

Onion Gravy: Skim fat from short-rib stock, reserving 3 tablespoons. Measure stock and add hot water to make 2 cups; set aside. Put 3 tablespoons reserved fat in skillet; add 4 cups sliced onions and cook till tender but not brown. Remove from heat.

Push onions to one side and blend 3 tablespoons enriched flour into fat. Slowly stir in meat stock. Return to heat and cook, stirring constantly, till gravy is bubbling all over. Add 1 teaspoon Worcestershire sauce and ½ teaspoon kitchen bouquet. Season with salt and pepper. Continue cooking slowly about 5 minutes, stirring now and then. Serve with braised short ribs.

Easy Onion Gravy: Skim fat from short-rib stock. Measure stock and add hot water to make 3 cups; pour into Dutch oven. Heat to boiling. Meanwhile thoroughly combine 3 tablespoons enriched flour with 1 envelope onion-soup mix. Gradually stir flour-onion mixture into hot stock; cook, stirring constantly till gravy thickens. Simmer about 7 minutes longer, stirring now and then.

Braised Short Ribs. Make gravy the traditional way, or short-cut with onion-soup mix.

Old-fashioned beef specials

Stuffed Flank Steaks

⅓ cup chopped onion
4 cups dry bread cubes
½ teaspoon salt
½ teaspoon poultry seasoning
Dash pepper
2 flank steaks (about 1¾ pounds total), scored
Enriched flour

• • •

1 1-pound can (2 cups) tomatoes
1 cup water
¼ cup chopped onion
¼ cup catsup

• • •

½ cup chopped green pepper
1 6-ounce can (1⅓ cups) broiled, sliced mushrooms

Cook ⅓ cup chopped onion in a little hot fat till golden; add bread cubes and seasonings; toss in skillet till bread is lightly toasted. Spread stuffing over steaks and roll as for jelly roll; fasten rolls with toothpicks and lace with string.

Roll in flour and brown on all sides in a little hot fat; sprinkle with salt and pepper. Add tomatoes, water, ¼ cup onion, and catsup. Cover; simmer 1¾ to 2 hours, or until tender; add green pepper, mushrooms and liquid last 15 minutes. Serves 6.

London Broil (*Broiled Flank Steak*)

1 flank steak (about 1½ pounds), scored
1 cup salad oil
1 tablespoon vinegar
1 clove garlic, minced

• • •

Salt and pepper

Select a *top-quality* flank steak. Place in shallow pan. Combine oil, vinegar, and garlic; pour over steak. Cover and let stand in refrigerator several hours or overnight, turning steak several times.

Preheat broiler. Broil steak 3 inches from heat about 5 minutes; season. Turn; broil 5 minutes more (for medium); season. Remove to heated platter. To serve, carve in *very thin* slices diagonally across grain. Makes 4 or 5 servings.

Fresh-brisket Feast

Place one 3 to 3½-pound fresh boneless beef brisket in Dutch oven; add 6 medium carrots, pared, 2 medium onions, halved, 2 stalks celery, 1 tablespoon salt, ¼ teaspoon pepper, and 10 whole cloves. Barely cover with water. Simmer covered 3 to 4 hours. About 45 minutes before meat is done, add 4 to 5 medium potatoes, pared and halved.

Transfer meat and vegetables to hot platter; keep hot. If desired, thicken broth to make gravy, or pass Horseradish Sauce. Slice meat across grain. Serves 8 to 10.

Fresh-brisket Feast

Long *gentle* cooking makes this cut tender. Sometime try cooking dumplings in the broth in place of the potatoes. →

Corned-beef Dinner

Company fare, this cut! Pair off with Irish potatoes and cabbage. Carve brisket across the grain, making thin slices. →

Corned-beef Dinner

3 to 4 pounds corned-beef brisket
2 onions, sliced
2 cloves garlic, minced
6 whole cloves
2 bay leaves
6 small to medium potatoes, pared
6 small carrots, pared
6 cabbage wedges (1 medium head)

Barely cover corned beef with hot water. Add onions, seasonings. Cover; simmer about 1 hour *per pound* of meat, or till tender. Remove meat from liquid; add potatoes, carrots. Cover; bring to boiling, cook 10 minutes. Add cabbage; cook 20 minutes more.

To glaze cooked meat, top with mustard, brown sugar, and ground cloves. Bake at 350° 15 to 20 minutes. Makes 6 servings.

Full of rich flavor—pork

Crown Roast of Pork

Have crown made at market from strip of pork loin (backbone removed) containing 10 to 14 ribs. Season with salt and pepper.

Place in roasting pan, bone ends up; wrap tips in foil to prevent excess browning. Insert meat thermometer so tip is in center of thick part of loin. Roast uncovered in slow oven (325°) till thermometer reads 185°, about 50 to 55 minutes *per pound* of meat. An hour before meat is done, fill center with Corn Stuffing.*

To serve roast, replace foil wraps with spiced crab apples or paper frills. To carve, slice between ribs. Serves 10 to 14.

Note: If stuffing isn't used, place roast in pan bone end down, so fat from roast bastes rib ends. At serving time, fill with Roast Potatoes (page 22) or other vegetables.

*Place any remaining stuffing in pan around roast, *or* place in greased casserole and dot with butter; cover; bake with roast for last hour of cooking time.

Corn Stuffing

1 1-pound can (2 cups) cream-style corn
1 12-ounce can (1½ cups) whole kernel corn, drained
1 beaten egg
1 cup soft bread crumbs
¼ cup chopped onion
¼ cup chopped green pepper
2 tablespoons chopped pimiento
1½ teaspoons salt
Dash pepper

Combine all ingredients. Fill center of Crown Roast of Pork about an hour before meat is done. Makes 1 quart.

Rolled Pork Loin Roast

Select boned and rolled pork loin roast. Season. Place fat side up on rack in open roasting pan. Insert meat thermometer; roast uncovered in slow oven (325°) until thermometer registers 185° (45 to 50 minutes *per pound* of meat).

Crown Roast of Pork, gala with spicy crab apples and colorful Corn Stuffing, is fare fit for a king!

Thick pork loin slices with fried-apple rings

Pork Loin Roast is extra-easy to carve. Just slice between the meaty ribs —each guest gets a "pork chop." Pass Pork Gravy for the mashed potatoes. Round out the meal with corn and coleslaw. Dessert: Squares of gingerbread.

Pork Loin Roast

Select a loin or rib pork roast. Have backbone loosened from ribs for easy carving. Rub salt, pepper, and a bit of sage over roast; place in open roasting pan with fat side up. Roast in slow oven (325°) till meat thermometer registers 185° (35 to 40 minutes *per pound* of meat). Make Pork Gravy (page 38) from the drippings.

Remove backbone in kitchen when roast is done. Serve with Glazed Apple Rings (page 42). Finish carving at table by cutting down between ribs.

Apple-glazed Pork Loin: Combine 1 tablespoon enriched flour, 1 teaspoon salt, 1 teaspoon dry mustard, ¼ teaspoon pepper. Rub mixture on meat. Roast as directed above. About 1 hour before roast is done, spread with mixture of 2 cups sweetened applesauce, ¼ cup brown sugar, ¼ teaspoon cinnamon, and ¼ teaspoon cloves. Return to oven till meat is done.

Loin roast is oven-ready in no time

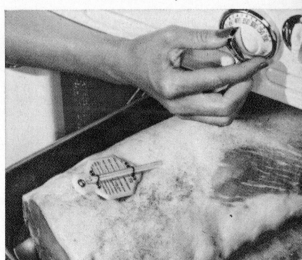

Place loin roast fat side up in shallow pan—ribs serve as rack. Season. Meat thermometer goes in at a slant, bulb in center of meat. Roast at 325° till well done (185° on thermometer).

For homespun treat, roast a Stuffed Pork Shoulder

A family favorite, this plump pork roast brimful of Herb Stuffing. Score top of meat for a pretty finish. Garnish platter with parsley and crab apples.

Stuffed Pork Shoulder

    4 to 5 pounds fresh boneless cushion shoulder
    Poultry seasoning
    Salt and pepper
    • • •
    1 recipe Herb Stuffing

BETTER HOMES AND GARDENS $ ECONOMY RECIPE $

Rub outside of meat and pocket with poultry seasoning; sprinkle with salt and pepper.

Lightly stuff with Herb Stuffing* (Cut pocket larger to hold more stuffing if desired.) Close opening with skewers and tie with cord.

Place meat fat side up on rack in shallow roasting pan (do not cover). Score top surface of meat, making shallow cuts. Roast in slow oven (325°) 40 to 45 minutes *per pound* (about 4 hours) or till pork is well done (no pink). Make Pork Gravy from pan drippings. Allow ⅓ pound meat per serving.

*Bake extra stuffing in greased pan or casserole the last hour of roasting. Baste occasionally with pork drippings.

Herb Stuffing

Toss together 4 cups dry bread cubes, 1 cup chopped celery, ½ cup chopped onion, 1½ teaspoons poultry seasoning or sage, 1¼ teaspoons salt, and ¼ teaspoon pepper.

Add ⅓ cup melted butter or margarine, then just enough hot water to moisten; mix lightly. Stuff pork shoulder.

Pork Gravy

Remove pork roast to warm platter; leave crusty bits in pan. Pour fat and meat juices into measuring cup; skim off fat.

For *each cup of gravy:* Measure 2 tablespoons of fat back into pan; blend in 2 tablespoons flour. Cook over low heat till frothy, stirring constantly. Remove from heat; add 1 cup liquid (meat juices, plus water if needed) and dash of kitchen bouquet. Stir smooth, return to heat, and cook till thick, stirring constantly and scraping pan to blend in crusty bits. Simmer about 5 minutes. Season.

Make spareribs your specialty

What ribs to buy? You'll find loin back and regular spareribs at the meat case.

Regular ribs have longer ribs at one end. Weight ranges from 1½ to 3 pounds. Cost is usually less than for loin back ribs.

Loin back ribs contain curved ribs of uniform length, weigh 1 to 1½ pounds.

Allow ¾ to 1 pound ribs per person.

Ribs with Onion Sauce

3 pounds spareribs, cut in pieces
2 cups onion slices
2 cloves garlic, minced
½ cup vinegar
½ cup water
¼ cup chili sauce
2 tablespoons lemon juice
2 tablespoons Worcestershire sauce
3 tablespoons brown sugar
1½ teaspoons salt
1 teaspoon dry mustard

Bake ribs in shallow pan at 450° for 30 minutes. Drain off excess fat. Meanwhile, cook onion and garlic in a little hot fat till tender; add remaining ingredients; simmer 10 minutes. Brush ribs with sauce. Reduce oven to 350°; bake 1½ hours or till well done, brushing occasionally with sauce.

Spareribs and Kraut

Brown spareribs in broiler; season and place over sauerkraut in baking dish. (Use 1 quart sauerkraut with 3 pounds ribs.)

Add ½ cup hot water; cover tightly and bake at 350° for 2½ to 3½ hours.

Barbecued Spareribs

3 to 4 pounds spareribs, cut in pieces
1 lemon, thinly sliced
1 large onion, thinly sliced
1 cup catsup
⅓ cup Worcestershire sauce
1 teaspoon chili powder
1 teaspoon salt
2 dashes Tabasco sauce
1½ cups water

Salt ribs. Place in shallow roasting pan, meaty side up. Roast in very hot oven (450°) 30 minutes. Drain excess fat from pan. Top each piece of ribs with a slice of unpeeled lemon and a slice of onion.

Combine remaining ingredients; bring to a boil and pour over ribs. Lower temperature control to 350°; bake till well done, about 1½ hours. Baste ribs with sauce every 15 minutes. If sauce gets too thick, add more water. Makes 4 servings.

A just-right sauce makes barbecued ribs best ever!

Take your pick of pork chops

Orange-glazed Pork Chops

    4 pork chops, about ¾ inch thick
    Salt and pepper
    ½ cup orange juice
    2 tablespoons brown sugar
    2 tablespoons orange marmalade
    1 tablespoon vinegar

Trim fat from chops. Heat fat in skillet; when you have about 1 tablespoon melted fat, remove trimmings. Brown chops on both sides in hot fat; season with salt and pepper. Drain off excess fat. Combine remaining ingredients; pour over chops. Cover; simmer 50 minutes or till chops are done—no pink. Remove chops to warm platter. Bring sauce to boiling; spoon over chops. Serves 4.

Pork Chops Cacciatora

    6 pork chops, about ¾ inch thick
    ½ teaspoon salt
    6 thin onion slices
    1 envelope spaghetti-sauce mix
    1 1-pound can (2 cups) tomatoes
    1 tablespoon brown sugar
    6 green pepper rings

Trim fat from chops. Brown chops in 1 tablespoon melted fat; season with salt and dash pepper; place in 11½x7½x1½-inch baking dish. Top each chop with onion slice. Combine next 3 ingredients; pour over chops. Cover with foil; bake at 350° for 1 hour. Uncover; top chops with pepper; bake 15 minutes. Serve with hot cooked rice. Serves 6.

Sauced or stuffed, pork chops fit many occasions.

Barbecued Pork and Bean Bake

Even Barbecued Pork Chops can be speedy—no browning of chops or mixing of sauce—

Place two 1-pound cans baked beans in tomato sauce in a 13x9x2-inch baking dish. Prepare 5 or 6 lean rib pork chops. For each chop: dash with salt and pepper; spread lightly with mustard; sprinkle with about 1½ tablespoons brown sugar; spread with about 1½ tablespoons catsup. Arrange chops over beans. With toothpick, attach 1 slice onion and ½ slice lemon to each chop.

Bake in a slow oven (325°) about 1½ hours or till pork chops are fork tender. Garnish with parsley. Serve with crisp relishes and hot, crusty bread. Makes 5 to 6 servings.

(Barbecued rib fans are sure to enjoy this recipe with loin back ribs substituted for pork chops. Cut in serving-size pieces; prepare according to directions above.)

Festive Fall Pork Chops

Meaty pork chops, slowly braised with dried fruits in sweet cider, are oh-so-tender. Perfect for fall meals—

6 pork chops, ½ inch thick

. . .

1½ cups apple cider or apple juice
1 tablespoon sugar
1 teaspoon salt
¼ teaspoon curry powder

. . .

6 dried prunes, pitted
12 dried apricot halves
2 tablespoons cornstarch
2 tablespoons water

Trim fat from chops; heat trimmings in skillet. When you have about 2 tablespoons melted fat, remove trimmings. Slowly brown pork chops on both sides in hot fat. Combine apple cider with sugar, salt, and curry powder; pour over chops. Place dried fruits on top of chops. Cover; cook over low heat about 1 hour or till chops are thoroughly cooked and fork-tender. Remove meat and fruit to a warm serving platter. Blend cornstarch with water; stir into pan juices. Cook and stir till mixture has thickened. Serve with pork chops and fruit. Makes 6 servings.

Pizza Pork Chops

Bonus—no prebrowning of chops—

6 double-rib pork chops, about
  1¼ inches thick
1 recipe Speedy Stuffing
1 5½- or 10½-ounce can pizza
  sauce
1 8-ounce can (1 cup)
  tomato sauce
3 slices sharp process cheese,
  halved diagonally

Have pocket cut *on bone side* of each chop. Trim off excess fat. Fill pockets with Stuffing. Season chops; place in shallow baker. Pour sauces over chops. Cover baker tightly with foil. Bake till done—no pink. Remove foil. Top with the cheese.

Speedy Stuffing: Mix ¼ to ½ teaspoon crushed oregano and ¼ cup chopped onion with 1 cup packaged herb-seasoned stuffing; prepare stuffing according to label directions, *but using only* ⅓ cup water and 2 tablespoons butter or margarine. Fill pork chops.

Cheese-stuffed Pork Chops

4 pork chops, 1 inch thick
1 3-ounce can (⅔ cup)broiled
  chopped mushrooms
¼ pound process Swiss cheese, diced
  (¾ cup)
¼ cup snipped parsley
½ teaspoon salt

. . .

½ cup fine dry bread crumbs.
¼ teaspoon salt
Dash pepper
1 beaten egg

Trim excess fat from chops. Cut a pocket in fat side of each chop (or have meatman do it). Drain mushrooms, reserving liquid. Combine mushrooms, cheese, parsley, and ½ teaspoon salt; stuff into pockets; toothpick and lace shut. Mix crumbs, ¼ teaspoon salt, and the pepper. Dip chops in egg, then in crumb mixture. Slowly brown chops in hot fat. Add reserved mushroom liquid; cover and simmer 1 hour or till chops are done—no pink. Remove chops.

Gravy: Blend 2 tablespoons all-purpose flour and ¼ cup cold water to a smooth paste; gradually stir flour mixture into liquid in skillet. Cook and stir till gravy thickens. Serves 4.

Zesty Barbecue Pork Chops

1 envelope tomato-soup mix
½ envelope or can (¼ cup) *dry*
  onion-soup mix
½ cup Italian salad dressing
2 tablespoons vinegar

. . .

2 cups water
2 tablespoons brown sugar
2 teaspoons Worcestershire sauce
1 teaspoon prepared horseradish
1 teaspoon prepared mustard

. . .

6 pork chops

In saucepan, combine tomato-soup mix, onion-soup mix, salad dressing, and vinegar; gradually stir in water. Add remaining ingredients, except pork chops. Bring to boiling; simmer 10 minutes. Brown chops in hot fat; add *1 cup* of the sauce. Simmer covered for 1 hour, basting occasionally. Add sauce as needed during cooking. Makes 6 servings.

Pork-chop Loaf

6 ¾-inch pork loin chops
Fat
1 cup chopped onion
1 cup chopped celery
¼ cup butter or margarine
4 cups bread cubes, partially dry
1 teaspoon salt
¼ teaspoon pepper
¼ teaspoon sage
¼ cup finely chopped parsley

Brown chops lightly in a little hot fat. Cook onion and celery in butter until golden but not brown. Combine remaining ingredients; add onion and celery. Place a chop fat side up at each end of a 10x5x3-inch loaf pan. Alternate chops and stuffing. Run skewers through chops. Bake in slow oven (325°) 1 hour, or till done. Makes 6 servings.

Glazed Apple Rings

Core apples, but do not pare. Cut in ½-inch slices. Brown lightly in butter or margarine. Sprinkle with granulated or brown sugar. Cover; cook over low heat till tender.

Baked Pork Chops with Prunes

6 thick pork chops
¼ cup catsup
¼ cup water
2 tablespoons lemon juice
1 teaspoon Worcestershire sauce
½ teaspoon dry mustard
1 small onion, sliced

Brown chops in small amount hot fat. Combine catsup, water, lemon juice. Worcestershire sauce, and mustard; pour over chops. Top with onion slices. Cover and bake in moderate oven (350°) *or* cook over low heat top of range 1 hour or till done. Serve with Spiced Prunes. Makes 6 servings.

Spiced Prunes

½ pound dried prunes, unpitted
1½ cups water
2 tablespoons vinegar
½ teaspoon cinnamon
3 whole cloves
2 tablespoons brown sugar

Simmer prunes in hot water 30 minutes or till tender. Add remaining ingredients and cook slowly 10 minutes more.

Pork Chops in Sour Cream

¾ teaspoon sage
½ teaspoon salt
Dash pepper
6 ½-inch loin pork chops
2 tablespoons fat
2 medium onions, sliced
1 beef bouillon cube
¼ cup boiling water
½ cup dairy sour cream
1 tablespoon flour
2 tablespoons snipped parsley

Combine sage, salt, and pepper; rub chops with the mixture. Brown chops lightly in hot fat. Drain off excess fat. Add onions to chops. Dissolve bouillon cube in boiling water; pour over chops. Cover and simmer 30 minutes. Remove chops from broth. Combine sour cream and flour; slowly stir in broth. Return mixture to skillet; heat to boiling. Serve gravy with chops; garnish with parsley. Serves 6.

Pork Steaks with Apple Stuffing

6 pork steaks, ½-inch thick
2 tablespoons fat
1 recipe Apple Stuffing
3 tart red apples, cored
   and halved

Slowly brown pork steaks on both sides in hot fat; season well with salt and pepper. Place in shallow baking dish; cover each steak with layer of Apple Stuffing, and top with apple half; sprinkle with sugar. Cover dish tightly with foil. Bake in moderate oven (350°) 1 hour or till pork is well done. Makes 6 servings.

Apple Stuffing

3 cups toasted bread cubes
1½ cups chopped unpared apples
½ cup seedless raisins
½ cup chopped celery
½ cup chopped onion
1 teaspoon salt
1 teaspoon poultry seasoning
¼ teaspoon pepper
½ cup canned condensed beef broth *or*
   1 beef bouillon cube dissolved in
   ½ cup hot water

Toss together bread cubes, chopped apple, raisins, celery, onion, and seasonings. Add beef broth or bouillon and toss lightly to moisten.

Pork cuts worth trying

Sweet-sour Pork

1½ pounds lean pork shoulder, cut in
    2x½-inch strips
1 No. 2 can (2½ cups)
    pineapple chunks
¼ cup brown sugar
2 tablespoons cornstarch
¼ cup vinegar
1 tablespoon soy sauce
½ teaspoon salt
¾ cup green-pepper strips
¼ cup thinly sliced onion
2 cans (about 5 cups) chow-mein noodles

BETTER HOMES AND GARDENS — ECONOMY RECIPE

Brown pork slowly in 2 tablespoons hot fat. Add ¼ cup water; cover and simmer till tender, about 1 hour.

Drain pineapple, reserving syrup. Combine brown sugar and cornstarch; add pineapple syrup, vinegar, soy sauce, and salt. Cook over low heat till thick, stirring constantly. Pour over hot, cooked pork; let stand 10 minutes or longer. Add pineapple, green pepper, onion. Cook 2 or 3 minutes; serve over noodles or rice. Makes 6 servings.

Tenderloin Patties in Cream

Have pork tenderloin cut into patties, or use pork cutlets. Sprinkle with flour, then season with salt, pepper. Brown in butter. For 8 patties add ½ cup light cream; cover, simmer about ½ hour or till done. Top with chopped parsley.

Baked-Stuffed Tenderloin

Select 2 pork tenderloins of equal size; have them split lengthwise and flattened.

Season. Spread Herb Stuffing (page 38) over one; lay the other on top and sew or skewer edges together. Season outside. Place 4 slices bacon over top.

Place on rack in open roasting pan; roast in slow oven (325°) 1½ hours.

Makes 8 servings.

Hocks 'n Kraut with Apple

2 1-pound cans sauerkraut
2 tablespoons brown sugar
½ teaspoon caraway seed
1 unpared large tart apple, sliced
1 medium onion, sliced
4 large smoked ham hocks
    (about 3 pounds)

With kitchen shears, snip through kraut several times while still in cans to cut up any long strips. In a greased 2-quart casserole, combine kraut, brown sugar, and caraway seed. Fold in apple slices. Layer onion slices over kraut mixture; top with ham hocks. Cover and bake in a slow oven (325°) for 3½ to 4 hours. Serve in casserole or, if desired, arrange on serving platter; garnish with parsley. Makes 4 servings.

To complete meal, serve buttered beets, a fresh spinach salad, and brown 'n serve rolls.

Hocks 'n Kraut with Apple. Good country-style cooking; a whole meal packed with flavor.

For tops in flavor, count on ham

Ham-carving secrets: *A bit of know-how and a razor-sharp knife*

1 Place shank end at carver's right. Cut a few slices from thin side (may be **near** or far side of ham).

2 Turn ham on flat surface cut. Hold with carving fork; remove small wedge 6 inches from shank end. Cut thin slices down to bone.

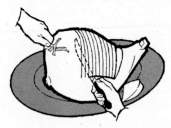

3 Run the knife along the leg bone as shown — the slices are released quickly and easily. Lift slices to one side of platter and serve.

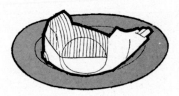

4 Time for seconds? Turn ham back to first position. Cut slices at right angles to bone; release by sliding knife along bone.

Ham at its best—*baked to perfection, scored on bias, topped with fruit glaze*

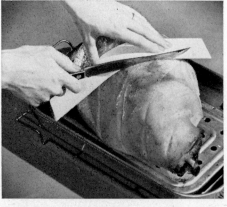

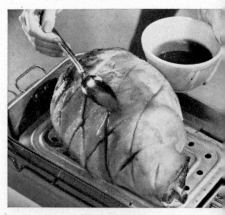

Place ham, fat side up, on rack in shallow baking pan. Insert meat thermometer in center of thickest part, tip not touching fat or bone.

Bake in slow oven (325°)—see timetable for cooking time.

Half an hour before end of cooking time, pour drippings from pan. Score ham fat in diamond pattern—cuts should be only ¼ inch deep, or they'll open too wide.

A strip of heavy paper, 12x2 inches, is an easy guide for cutting parallel lines.

Spoon glaze* over ham till evenly coated. Now it goes back into oven for 30 minutes. For heavier coating, spoon glaze over several times.

Quick Glazes: Orange marmalade or apricot preserves. See next page.

Festive Baked Ham. Pipe on softened cream cheese to outline scoring when ham is cool; make paper doily frill.

Baked Ham

Place 12- to 14-pound whole ham fat side up on rack in shallow pan. Insert meat thermometer as shown at left. Bake in slow oven (325°)—see timetable for baking time and internal temperature for the kind of ham (uncooked or cooked) you've chosen.

Half an hour before ham is done, remove from oven and pour fat drippings from pan. Score ham as shown. Spoon marmalade, preserves, or one of glazes below, over ham. Continue baking 30 minutes or till well glazed.

Allow ½ to ¾ pound uncooked-type ham per serving, ⅓ pound fully-cooked or ready-to-eat type.

Crab apple Glaze: Combine 1 cup brown sugar and ½ cup syrup from canned spiced crab apples. Heat and stir. Spoon half of glaze over ham. Bake 15 minutes; spoon on remaining glaze, place crab apples on rack with ham; bake 15 minutes more.

Tangy Mustard Glaze: Mix 1 cup brown sugar, 1 teaspoon dry mustard, 2 to 3 tablespoons drippings. Glaze clove-studded ham.

Honey Glaze: Mix ½ cup honey, 1 cup brown sugar, ½ cup orange juice. Glaze.

Baked-ham timetable

Set oven at 325°. Times are for chilled hams taken right from refrigerator—

Uncooked (cook-before-eating type)	Time (per lb.)	Time* (total)
Half ham, 6-8 lbs. 8-lb., for example	25 min.	3 hrs.
10-12-lb. ham 10-lb., for example	18-20 min.	3½ hrs.
12-14-lb. ham 12-lb., for example	16-18 min.	3¾ hrs.
14-16 lbs. and over	14-16 min.	3¾ hrs.
Boned, rolled half ham 8-lb., for example	30 min.	4 hrs.
whole ham 10-lb., for example	25 min.	4 hrs.

*Cooking times are approximate only. If you use a meat thermometer, cook ham to an internal temperature of 160°.

Cooked (fully-cooked type)	Time (per lb.)	Time† (total)
Half ham, 6-8 lbs. 8-lb., for example	18-24 min.	2½ hrs.
Whole ham, 12-14 lbs. 12-lb., for example	12-15 min.	3 hrs.
Boned, rolled half ham 8-lb., for example	20 min.	2½ hrs.
whole ham 12-14-lb., for example	18 min.	4 hrs.

†Cooking times are approximate only. If you use a meat thermometer, heat to 130°.

← Whole ham gets one last basting with Pineapple Glaze (page 47) as it grills to a turn on the rotisserie. Another good bet for the rotisserie—round boneless ham.

The butt *end* and the shank *end* are the pieces left after the more expensive center slices have been removed. The end pieces may be baked. Or you can have the butt end sliced for broiling or pan-frying. With the shank end, you can cut off and slice the top part for frying. Use the rest in casseroles.

Boneless ham. Some retain the ham shape, others are formed into a long roll—both kinds make dandy rotisserie roasts. (See picture on page 150.)

Smoked picnic is a pork shoulder cured like ham. You can buy either the fully cooked or cook-before-eating type. It comes bone in or boned. Smaller than ham and less expensive, picnic may be a budget choice.

Do you know these hams?

Country-style or **Tennessee ham** is real old-fashioned Southern ham. Its heavy cure gives zesty flavor, firm texture. Directions for soaking and cooking come with it.

Virginia or **Smithfield ham** is flat-shaped, has a distinctive flavor. Instructions for preparing are in cloth bag. Slice this ham tissue-paper thin.

Proscuitto, Italian-style ham, is highly flavored—must be sliced paper-thin. It's air-dried, aged in spices, and covered with crushed black pepper. This ham isn't cooked and you don't cook it either! The way it's cured and aged makes it safe to eat as is.

Read label on ham carefully

When you shop for ham, you'll notice two kinds—the *fully cooked* type and the *cook-before-eating* type. Both are tender, modern smoked hams. It's important to know which kind you are buying—if the label has been removed from a slice or piece of ham, ask your meatman.

You may see *"tenderized"* or *"tendered"* on the ham label. All modern-style hams are smoked to a higher internal temperature, and are therefore tender compared to the products our parents knew.

Fully cooked ham—you may serve it chilled, just as is, or heat it in the oven until meat thermometer reaches 130°.

Cook-before-eating ham means just that. Bake to internal temperature of 160°.

Canned ham is fully cooked and may be served as it comes from the can. Some canned ham is hickory smoked for old-time flavor. Even though canned, the ham may need to be stored in the refrigerator—check the label to be sure.

Half-ham makes a good choice for the small family. The butt half (the top piece) is meatier than the shank half of a short-shank style ham.

Italian Picnic Shoulder

1 whole picnic shoulder,
   about 5 pounds
6 to 8 cloves garlic
¾ cup vinegar

Remove skin from picnic. Peel, slice garlic cloves in fourths lengthwise. Cut vertical slits about ½ inch deep in meat and insert garlic slices as you remove knife. Place in big kettle, cover picnic with water, and add vinegar. Cover; simmer about 1 hour and 40 minutes (20 minutes per pound). Remove from broth. Bake in slow oven (300°) about 50 minutes (10 minutes per pound).

Baked Picnic Shoulder

Picnics may be baked and glazed like ham of the same type. Follow directions on page 45, or label instructions.

Rotisserie-roasted Ham

Buy a whole ham or round boneless ham. The amount will depend on the crowd. If ham has casing, slit lengthwise with sharp knife and remove. Score ham. Center lengthwise on spit; adjust in rotisserie.

Cooking time varies with the type and amount of heat (electric or charcoal), size and shape of ham. Depend on your meat thermometer to tell when it's done. *Cooked* ham (fully cooked or ready-to-eat type) needs an internal temperature of 130 degrees; *uncooked* ham needs 160 degrees.

The last 30 minutes, brush ham occasionally with *Pineapple Glaze:* Combine ½ cup brown sugar, ½ cup unsweetened pineapple juice, ¼ cup vinegar, and 1 tablespoon prepared mustard; simmer uncovered 10 minutes. Pass any leftover glaze.

Broiled Ham or Picnic Slice

Select 1-inch ham slice; trim rind, if any. Slash edge in several places. Broil 2 inches from heat; turn once. Broil *cooked* slice (ready-to-eat or fully cooked) 15 minutes; *uncooked-type* slice 25 minutes.

Pan-broiled Ham or Picnic Slice

Choose ¼- to ½-inch-thick slices of smoked ham or picnic. Rub heavy skillet with ham fat. Over low heat, pan-broil ½-inch slice *ready-to-eat* or *fully cooked* ham 3 to 4 minutes each side; ½-inch slice *uncooked-type* ham 8 minutes each side.

Cranberry-stuffed Ham Slices

Score edges of two ½-inch smoked ham slices; stud with whole cloves. Place 1 ham slice in 10x6x1½-inch baking dish; spread with *half* of one 1-pound can whole-cranberry sauce. Top with other ham slice, then remaining cranberry sauce.

Bake at 350° 45 minutes for *ready-to-eat* or *fully cooked* ham; 1 hour for *uncooked-type* ham. Drain. Makes 6 servings.

Broiled Ham and Limas

1 slice smoked ham, ¾ to 1 inch thick
2 cups hot cooked or canned green Limas
2 cups shredded process American cheese

Score fat edge of ham slice; broil 3 to 5 inches from heat—5 minutes each side for *ready-to-eat* or *fully cooked* ham, 10 minutes each side for *uncooked-type* ham. Drain Limas; pile atop ham; sprinkle with cheese. Reduce heat; low-broil till cheese melts.

Fast meal—
Broiled
Ham and Limas

It's mealtime in no time at all!

Cooked ham slice, canned yams and fruit give you head start on supper

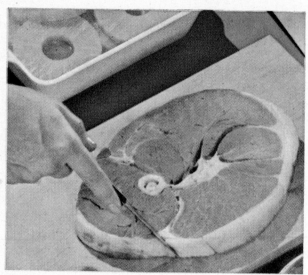

For this speedy meal, call on your broiler. Select a ¾-inch *cooked* ham slice (ready-to-eat type). Score edge of ham slice about ¼ inch deep in several places to keep slice from cupping while it broils—don't cut into meat.

(If you choose an uncooked ham slice, broil it 10 minutes on one side; turn, add pineapple slices and canned sweet potatoes, and broil 10 minutes longer.)

Place ham slice, canned sweet-potato halves, and pineapple rings on broiler rack. Brush the potatoes and pineapple with melted butter or margarine. Place foods 3 inches from heat.

(Preheat broiler or not, according to range instructions.) Broil 5 minutes, then turn ham. Place a canned spiced crab apple in center of each pineapple ring. Brush potatoes and pineapple with the melted butter. Broil 5 minutes more.

Marmalade-glazed Ham Slices

Easy for company! "No-carve" baked ham boasts luscious orange flavor

Cut four ¾-inch-thick slices from a boneless roll-shaped fully cooked ham. It's trimmed, a snap to slice evenly.

Remember this boneless ham for coldmeat platters, Dutch-lunch sandwiches, too. Just slice, and it's ready to serve.

Drained canned pineapple slices, one for each ham slice, make delicious baked-on garnish. Cut the pineapple rings in half. To start, arrange two pieces at end of an 11½x7½x1½-inch baking dish to form scallops. Overlap with ham slice.

Repeat "stairsteps" of pineapple and ham. Halve 4 canned or cooked sweet potatoes; arrange along one side of ham. Spoon orange marmalade over all. Bake at 325°—takes only 45 minutes.

Hurry-up ham meal broils to a tasty turn

While the ham sizzles to perfection, fix chilly crisp salad platter of carrot sticks, cauliflowerets, and pickled beets. Dessert? Spoon strawberries over sponge-cake cups and top with whipped cream.

Use wide spatula to lift ham dinner from baking dish onto hot platter; add dabbles of marmalade, parsley.

Smoked pork shoulder—so delicious even company won't guess you're tightening the purse strings.

Pork treats to bring compliments

Smoked Pork Dinner

1 2- to 2½-pound smoked
   boneless shoulder butt
Prepared mustard
Onion slices
Whole cloves
1 1-pound 2-ounce can
   vacuum-pack sweet potatoes
½ cup brown sugar

BETTER HOMES AND GARDENS ECONOMY RECIPE

Place meat in deep kettle and cover with cold water. Bring just to boiling; reduce heat and simmer (*do not boil*) about 1 hour *per pound* or till tender. Lift from water.

Make 5 diagonal slashes ¾ way through meat; spread cut surfaces with mustard; insert onion slice in each slash. Spread top of meat with mustard and stud with cloves. Arrange sweet potatoes around meat. Sieve brown sugar over meat and potatoes.

Bake in moderate oven (350°) 30 minutes or till meat is glazed and potatoes are hot. Carve pork in thin slices. Makes 8 servings.

Broiled or Pan-broiled Canadian-style Bacon

To broil: Place ¼-inch slices Canadian-style bacon on broiler rack. Broil 3 inches from heat about 5 minutes on each side.

To pan-broil: Preheat skillet. Brown ⅛- to ¼-inch slices on both sides, then reduce heat and finish cooking.

Baked Canadian-style Bacon

2 pounds Canadian-style bacon, in
   one piece
½ cup brown sugar
½ teaspoon dry mustard
½ cup unsweetened pineapple juice

Place bacon in shallow baking pan. Combine sugar, mustard, and pineapple juice for glaze; spread over bacon. Bake uncovered in slow oven (325°) 1 hour. Baste bacon with glaze every 15 minutes. Makes 8 servings. Or spread this type bacon with one of the glazes for ham—see pages 44 and 45.

From the ham bone—hearty soup and stew

Old-fashioned Split-pea Soup

1 pound (2¼ cups) green
   split peas
2½ quarts water
1 meaty ham bone
1½ cups sliced onion
½ teaspoon pepper
¼ teaspoon garlic salt
¼ teaspoon marjoram
1 cup diced celery
1 cup sliced carrots

Cover peas with water; soak overnight, or boil peas gently in water 2 minutes and soak 1 hour. Drain. Add 2½ quarts water, ham bone, onion, and seasonings. Bring to a boil, cover, reduce heat, simmer 2 hours. Stir occasionally. Remove bone; cut off meat. Return meat to soup; add remaining ingredients. Cook slowly 45 minutes. Salt to taste. Makes 8 to 10 servings.

Kettle-of-beans Stew

1½ cups dried navy beans

• • •

1 medium onion, sliced
1 ham bone or pieces of
   leftover ham
Water
Salt
Pepper

Thoroughly wash the navy beans. Cover with cold water and let soak several hours or overnight. Drain.

To beans, add onion, ham bone or left-over ham, and water to cover. Heat to boiling; reduce heat.

Cover and simmer until beans are tender, about 1½ to 2 hours. Remove bone; cut off meat (if any) and return to stew. Season to taste. Makes 4 servings.

Bacon—skillet-fried, oven-baked or broiled

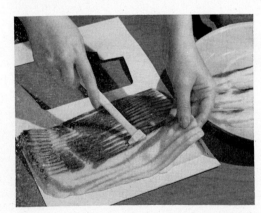

Separate bacon slices with rubber spatula — it's a snap even when they're cold. Slip spatula under end of bacon slice and "slither" lengthwise, lifting and removing each slice.

To broil bacon, separate slices and place on rack of broiler pan. Broil 3 to 5 inches from heat; turn only once. No need to drain. Bacon cooks quickly, so watch closely.

To fry bacon, put bacon strips in unheated skillet. Fry over moderately low heat for 6 to 8 minutes, turning frequently. Drain. Crisp bacon? Spoon fat off during cooking.

Oven-bake — that's the easy way to cook bacon for a crowd. Place separated slices on rack in shallow baking pan. Bake at 400° for 10 minutes. Needs no turning or draining.

Put Spring in meals with lamb

Roast Stuffed Shoulder of Lamb. Rolled inside is savory bread stuffing. Outside's prettied with bacon strips—a flavor plus. Platter partner: juicy pear halves filled with mint jelly.

Roast Stuffed Shoulder of Lamb

Select 3- to 3½-pound boned lamb shoulder. Rub outside surface with salt and pepper. Place Savory Stuffing on rib side. Roll meat and fasten with skewers; lace securely with string. Place on rack in shallow pan. Roast in slow oven (325°) about 2 hours, or 40 minutes *per pound* of meat.

About 30 minutes before roast is done, lay bacon strips over meat. Remove string and skewers before carving. Makes 6 servings.

Savory Stuffing: Combine 4 cups ½-inch dry bread cubes, 3 tablespoons chopped onion, 1 teaspoon salt, ½ teaspoon poultry seasoning, ¼ teaspoon pepper. Add ⅓ cup melted butter or margarine, and ¼ cup hot water; toss gently to mix.

Roast Leg of Lamb

Select leg of lamb—French or American.* Without removing fell (paper-like covering), season meat. A clove of garlic may be inserted in leg. Place fat side up on rack in open roasting pan. If fat covering is very thin, lay bacon strips over cut side. Insert meat thermometer in thickest part, tip not touching fat or bone.

Roast in slow oven (325°) 30 to 35 minutes *per pound* or till meat thermometer registers 175° for medium, 180° for well done. Makes 8 to 10 servings.

*French leg: Meat is trimmed from end of leg bone. *American leg:* Leg bone is cut short; meat is wrapped over the end and skewered to make compact roast.

any time of year

Roast Lamb Shoulder Roll

3 tablespoons enriched flour
1 tablespoon dry mustard
½ teaspoon salt
¼ teaspoon pepper
½ cup cold water

. . .

4- to 5-pound lamb shoulder,
  boned and rolled
1 cup currant or mint jelly

Mix flour and seasonings; add water and blend. Spread over lamb shoulder. Place on rack in open roasting pan. Insert meat thermometer with tip not resting in fat. Roast in slow oven (325°) 45 minutes *per pound* or till meat thermometer registers 180° (for well done). Spread with jelly the last hour; baste every 15 minutes. Serves 8 to 10.

Lamb-chop Grill

5 1-inch lamb chops
Tiny canned or cooked potatoes
Melted butter

. . .

1 8-ounce package brown-and-serve
  sausage

. . .

2 tomatoes
½ cup soft bread crumbs
¼ cup shredded process American cheese

. . .

10 bacon slices

Score fat edge of each chop. String potatoes on skewers and brush with butter. Place chops and potatoes on broiler-pan rack. Broil 4 inches from heat 10 minutes. Season chops and potatoes; turn. Add sausage links; broil 5 minutes. Meanwhile, halve tomatoes; score cut surfaces, making ½-inch squares. Mix crumbs and cheese; sprinkle on tomatoes.

Arrange tomatoes and bacon slices on broiler rack. Turn sausage. Butter potatoes again—dash with paprika. Broil about 5 minutes more or till bacon is done.

***Tasty-Lamb-chop Grill
is easy on the cook!***

Dinner's ready—broiler fast! This mixed grill is just right for four hungry people (give Dad the extra lamb chop). Buttery potatoes and cheese-topped tomatoes broil along with thick lamb chops, bacon, and sausage links.

Crown Roast of Lamb

Have meatman prepare crown of 10 to 16 ribs. Wrap rib ends with foil to prevent charring. Season; place bone ends up on rack in open roasting pan.

Fill with Savory Stuffing*, page 52. Roast at 325° for 30 to 35 minutes *per pound*.

Replace foil with paper frills. To carve, slice between ribs.

*If stuffing isn't used, place roast upside down in roasting pan so fat from roast bastes rib ends. At serving time, fill center with cooked new peas, or tiny carrots, or a whole cooked cauliflower.

Broiled Lamb Chops

Have loin, rib, or shoulder chops cut ¾- to 1-inch thick. Place in broiler 3 inches from heat. When brown, season; turn and brown other side.

Allow total broiling time of 12 to 15 minutes for chops 1-inch thick.

Lamb Chops Oriental

6 lamb shoulder chops,
  ½-inch thick

• • •

½ cup soy sauce
½ cup water
1 clove garlic, minced

• • •

6 canned peach halves
Mint jelly

Score fat edges of chops. Place in shallow baking dish. Combine soy sauce, water, and garlic; pour over chops. Let stand in refrigerator several hours or overnight.

Arrange the marinated chops on broiler-pan rack. Broil 3 inches from heat about 10 minutes on first side.

Turn chops, then place peaches, hollow side up, in broiler with chops. Broil 5 to 8 minutes longer, filling peach halves with jelly toward end of broiling time.

Makes 6 servings.

Lamb Chops Oriental. The soy-sauce marinade gives exciting new flavor to penny-wise shoulder chops—makes them company special. Jelly-filled peach halves grill along with meat.

For an interesting twist to popular leg of lamb roast, try Lamb West Indies. A subtle blend of coffee, cream, port, and currant jelly bastes the meat as it cooks, and lifts it to epicurean heights.

Sweet 'n Sour Lamb Chops

  4 lamb shoulder chops, about
    1 inch thick
  ¼ cup *each* vinegar and brown sugar
  1 teaspoon salt
  Dash pepper
  ½ teaspoon ground ginger
  4 slices orange
  4 wedges lemon
  1 tablespoon cornstarch

Brown chops over low heat. Combine vinegar, brown sugar, salt, dash pepper, and ginger; pour over meat. Top each chop with orange slice and lemon wedge. Cover; cook over low heat 30 minutes or till tender. Remove to warm platter. Pour pan juices into measuring cup; skim off fat; add water to make 1 cup. Return liquid to skillet. Blend cornstarch and 1 tablespoon water; stir into liquid. Cook and stir till mixture boils. Serve over chops on fluffy rice. Serves 4.

Leg of Lamb West Indies

Cut 2 or 3 slits in a 5- to 6-pound leg of lamb without removing thin paper-like covering; insert 1 clove garlic, sliced. Mix 1 teaspoon *each* ground ginger and dry mustard; rub over lamb. Place, fat side up, on rack in shallow roasting pan. Insert meat thermometer so tip reaches center of largest muscle. Roast at 325° for 3 to 3½ hours or till meat thermometer registers 180°. After first hour of roasting, dissolve 2 teaspoons sugar in 1 cup hot strong coffee; stir in 2 tablespoons *each* light cream and port wine; pour over lamb. Baste occasionally during remainder of roasting. Lift meat to warm platter. Pour pan juices into 2-cup measure; skim off fat. Add water to make 1½ cups. Measure 2 tablespoons fat back into pan; blend in 2 tablespoons flour; stir in meat juices and ⅓ cup currant jelly. Cook and stir till thick. Season to taste. Pass sauce with lamb.

Lamb—sauced, skewered, or in stew

Barbecued Lamb Riblets

3 to 4 pounds lamb riblets
1 lemon, sliced
¾ cup catsup
¾ cup water
½ cup chopped onion
2 tablespoons brown sugar
3 tablespoons Worcestershire sauce
1 tablespoon vinegar
1½ teaspoons monosodium glutamate
¾ teaspoon salt
Dash Tabasco sauce

Brown riblets (cut in serving pieces) slowly in skillet. Spoon off drippings. Season; top with lemon slices. Combine remaining ingredients; pour over meat. Cover and simmer 1½ hours or till tender. Remove excess fat. Serve with the sauce. Makes 4 to 6 servings.

Zippy Lamb Shanks

2 medium onions, sliced
1 clove garlic, minced
1 cup sliced celery
1 cup catsup
1 cup water
1 tablespoon
    Worcestershire sauce
4 lamb shanks

Combine all ingredients except lamb for the sauce. Cover and simmer 5 to 10 minutes.

Season lamb shanks with salt and pepper and brown in small amount hot fat. Add sauce. Cover and simmer 1½ hours or till tender. Or, cover and bake in slow oven (325°) about 2 hours or till done. Makes 4 servings.

Barbecued Lamb Riblets The delicately flavored barbecue sauce does great things for bargain lamb riblets; the lemon slices add lots of tang.

Garlic Lamb Kabobs

1½ pounds boneless lamb shoulder,
  cut in 1-inch cubes
1 cup garlic salad dressing, *or*
  1 envelope garlic dressing mix*
2 medium green peppers, cut in squares
1 1-pound can (2 cups) small onions

Place meat in shallow dish; pour dressing over. Let stand, turning occasionally, 2 hours at room temperature or overnight in refrigerator. Run eight 12-inch skewers through meat fat. String kabobs in this order: lamb, green pepper, lamb, onion. Broil 4 inches from heat 10 to 15 minutes, turning once. Brush occasionally with dressing.

*Prepare mix according to label directions.

Curried Lamb

Gourmet flavor from budget cuts—

2 pounds lean lamb breast or shoulder,
  cubed
2 tablespoons fat

1½ teaspoons salt
1 bay leaf
6 whole black peppers
1 medium onion, sliced
1 teaspoon chopped parsley

. . .

¼ cup enriched flour
1 teaspoon curry powder
3 tablespoons cold water

. . .

Hot cooked rice
Curry accompaniments

Brown meat slowly in hot fat; cover meat with boiling water (about 2 cups); add salt, bay leaf, whole peppers, onion, and parsley. Cover and cook slowly 1½ hours, or until meat is tender.

Remove meat and measure 2 cups stock, adding water if necessary. Mix flour and curry powder; slowly stir in cold water and blend. Stir into stock; cook, stirring constantly, until mixture thickens. Add meat and heat.

Serve with fluffy rice. Offer little bowls of curry accompaniments—plumped raisins, peanuts, flaked coconut, chutney, or watermelon pickles. Makes 6 servings.

Favorite Lamb Stew

1½ pounds lean boneless lamb shoulder,
  cut in 1-inch cubes
3 cups water
1 clove garlic, minced
2 teaspoons salt
¼ teaspoon pepper
4 carrots, cut in 2-inch lengths
6 tiny onions
3 small potatoes, halved
1 10-ounce package frozen peas
2 tablespoons minced parsley

Flour meat; brown in small amount hot fat. Add next 4 ingredients. Cover; simmer (don't boil) 1½ hours or till meat is almost tender. Add carrots, onions, and potatoes; cook done, about 20 minutes. Add peas and parsley. Cook 5 minutes or till done. Season to taste. Makes 5 to 6 servings.

Braised Mutton Chops

Mutton is stronger flavored than lamb. Brown ½-inch chops in hot fat, season; add water and simmer 1½ hours or till done.

Pot Roast of Mutton

Select leg or shoulder roast of mutton. Trim excess fat from roast; heat fat in large skillet or Dutch oven. Insert several cloves of garlic in roast. Slowly brown meat on all sides in hot fat. Sprinkle with salt and pepper. Add 1 cup tomato juice or water and ½ teaspoon curry powder. Cover; cook slowly 45 minutes *per pound* or till tender. Add more juice or water, if needed.

Delicately flavored veal—give

Veal Roast

Select bone-in veal roast from leg, loin, rump, or shoulder; or a boned, rolled rump or shoulder roast.

Sprinkle with salt and pepper, and place, fat side up, on rack in open roasting pan. Lay slices of bacon or salt pork over top. Insert meat thermometer in thickest part of roast, tip not touching bone or fat. Roast in slow oven (325°) 35 to 40 minutes *per pound* for bone-in roasts, or 45 to 50 minutes *per pound* for boned, rolled roasts. Thermometer will register 170° when done.

Make gravy from drippings, following recipe for Perfect Gravy, page 93.

Braised Rolled Veal Shoulder

Brown rolled veal shoulder on all sides in hot fat. Season with salt and pepper. Place on rack in roasting pan and add small amount of water. Cover and cook in slow oven (325°) until tender, allowing 45 minutes *per pound*. Vegetables may be added last 45 minutes.

Roast Stuffed Breast of Veal

8 ounces (1 cup) bulk pork sausage
1 cup soft medium bread crumbs
1 cup medium cracker crumbs
1 cup chopped tart apple
2 tablespoons chopped onion
¾ cup hot water
½ teaspoon salt
Dash pepper
. . .
1 veal breast (about 3 pounds), boned
Salt
Bacon slices

Fry sausage lightly; do not drain. Add next 7 ingredients and mix for stuffing.

Sprinkle inside surface of veal with salt. Top half the veal with stuffing. Fold other half over stuffing and fasten together with metal skewers. Place on rack in shallow roasting pan; lay bacon slices on top to cover veal. Do not cover pan or add water. Roast in slow oven (325°) about 3 hours or till well done—no pink. Makes 6 servings.

City Chicken

2 pounds boneless veal shoulder,
    cut in 1½-inch cubes
½ cup *fine* cracker crumbs
½ cup corn-flake crumbs
1 teaspoon salt
1 teaspoon paprika
¾ teaspoon poultry seasoning or thyme
½ teaspoon monosodium glutamate
Dash pepper
1 slightly beaten egg
2 tablespoons milk
2 to 3 tablespoons fat
1 chicken bouillon cube

Push veal cubes onto 6 skewers. Combine cracker and corn-flake crumbs and seasonings. Combine egg and milk. Dip meat in egg mixture, then in crumbs. Brown slowly on all sides in hot fat. Dissolve bouillon cube in ¾ cup hot water, add to meat. Cover tightly; simmer 1 hour or till tender*. Serve meat liquid as gravy. Makes 6 servings.

*Or cover and bake in moderate oven (350°) 1 hour or till tender.

Tasty veal fix-up—City Chicken

Cubes of veal shoulder get rolled in crumbs after a dip in egg—result? Crusty City Chicken at right.

Brown the crumb-coated veal, add bouillon, and cook tender. The gravy makes itself—crumbs are the thickening. A good electric skillet special.

t gentle cooking

Breaded Veal Cutlets

2 pounds veal round steak, ½ to
    ¾ inch thick
Salt and pepper

• • •

1 cup corn-flake crumbs
2 slightly beaten eggs
2 tablespoons water

• • •

⅛ cup fat
1 cup milk
1 can condensed cream of mushroom
    soup

Cut veal into 6 pieces; season. Dip into
the corn-flake crumbs, then into egg mixed
with water, and again into crumbs.

Brown meat in hot fat. Mix milk with
soup; pour over veal. Cover; bake in 300°
oven 1 hour or till tender. Makes 6 servings.

Veal Chops

Select 4 to 6 veal chops, ¾ to 1 inch
thick. Dip in flour*; brown in hot fat, season with salt, pepper. Add small amount of
water, cover, cook slowly about 45 minutes.
Allow one chop per serving.

*Or dip chops into mixture of one slightly
beaten egg and 1 tablespoon water, then
into fine cracker or dry bread crumbs.

Veal Chops Hawaiian

4 ¾-inch veal loin or rib chops
Salt and pepper
4 slices canned pineapple
4 dried prunes
8 medium carrots
½ cup hot water

Brown chops in hot fat; season. Place pineapple slice on each chop, prune in center.
Add carrots and water; cover and cook
slowly 1½ hours. Makes 4 servings.

Veal with an American or a foreign flair

Savory steak and stuffing

Plump Veal Birds line up on the chop plate. There's savory bread stuffing rolled inside each tender piece of meat. (Recipe on next page.) Go-withs: Glazed whole baby carrots and pimiento-dotted whole kernel corn.

Veal Steak with Sauce

¼ cup enriched flour
1 teaspoon salt
1 teaspoon paprika
½ teaspoon poultry seasoning
¼ teaspoon pepper
1½ pounds veal steak, cut in serving pieces
2 tablespoons fat
1 cup soft bread crumbs
2 tablespoons butter or margarine, melted
½ cup grated Parmesan cheese
¼ cup sesame seed, toasted
½ cup hot water
1 can condensed cream of chicken soup
½ teaspoon monosodium glutamate
1 cup dairy sour cream

Combine flour and seasonings; dip meat in mixture. Brown slowly in hot fat; reserve drippings. Arrange meat in 10x6x1½-inch baking dish. Combine bread crumbs, butter, cheese, and sesame seed; spoon over meat. Stir water into meat drippings; pour around meat. Bake in moderate oven (350°) 45 to 50 minutes, or till meat is tender.

Serve with *Sour-cream Sauce:* Heat and stir chicken soup. Blend in remaining ingredients; heat through. Makes 6 servings.

Paprika Wiener Schnitzel

1½ pounds veal steak or cutlets, ½- to ¾-inch thick
1 medium onion, thinly sliced
1 clove garlic, minced
2 tablespoons fat

• • •

¼ cup enriched flour
1 teaspoon salt
¼ teaspoon pepper

• • •

1 cup dairy sour cream
⅓ cup condensed consomme *or* 1 bouillon cube dissolved in ⅓ cup hot water
1 tablespoon paprika
3 drops Tabasco sauce

Cut meat in serving pieces; pound till about double in area. Cook onion and garlic in hot fat till onion is tender but not brown; remove from skillet.

Dip pounded veal steak in flour seasoned with salt and pepper; brown on both sides in hot fat. Add cooked onion and garlic to meat in skillet; cover and cook slowly 15 minutes, or till meat is tender.

Combine remaining ingredients and pour over meat. Cover tightly and simmer 10 to 15 minutes longer. Makes 4 servings.

Veal Birds

2 pounds ½-inch veal steak
1¼ teaspoons salt
Dash pepper

. . .

3 cups dry bread cubes
3 tablespoons butter, melted
2½ tablespoons chopped onion
¾ teaspoon salt
½ teaspoon poultry seasoning
Dash pepper

Cut steak in serving pieces. Pound thoroughly with meat pounder till double in area; sprinkle with salt and pepper.

To make stuffing, combine remaining ingredients; add enough water to moisten (about 2 teaspoons). Top veal with stuffing. Roll as for jelly roll; fasten with toothpicks.

Brown in hot fat; add ⅓ cup hot water; cover tightly and cook slowly 1 hour or till tender, turning occasionally.

Makes 6 servings.

Sweet-sour Veal With Rice

1 No. 2 can (2½ cups) pineapple tidbits
1½ pounds veal, cut in 1½-inch cubes
2 tablespoons fat
1 cup celery slices
½ cup chopped onion
¾ teaspoon salt
Dash pepper
1 beef bouillon cube
½ cup hot water

. . .

1 1-pound can (2 cups) bean sprouts, drained
1 3-ounce can (⅔ cup) broiled sliced mushrooms

. . .

3 tablespoons cornstarch
3 tablespoons soy sauce
1 teaspoon monosodium glutamate

. . .

3 cups hot cooked rice

Drain pineapple, reserving syrup. Brown veal in hot fat. Add celery, onion, salt, pepper, bouillon cube dissolved in hot water, and the reserved pineapple syrup.

Cover: simmer 60 to 75 minutes or till meat is tender. Add pineapple, bean sprouts, mushrooms, and mushroom liquid.

Blend cornstarch with soy sauce and monosodium glutamate; stir into hot mixture. Cook, stirring constantly, until thick. Serve over rice. Makes 6 servings.

Surprise Veal Roll-ups

6 ¼-inch veal cutlets
3 thin slices boiled ham, cut in half
½ cup shredded sharp process American cheese
¼ cup chopped stuffed green olives
¼ cup cooking sherry

Pound cutlets with meat pounder till about double in area; sprinkle with pepper. Put one piece of ham on each cutlet.

Mix cheese and chopped olives; spread over ham. Roll veal as for jelly roll; fasten with toothpicks or tie with cord.

Brown meat in butter; cook uncovered over low heat 30 minutes or till tender, turning occasionally to prevent sticking.

Add cooking sherry and heat through. Makes 6 servings.

Sweet-sour Veal With Rice boasts delicious Oriental flavor. Veal cubes, mushrooms, bean sprouts, pineapple tidbits—they all take well to soy sauce. Pass extra soy sauce for seasoning to taste.

Veal Scaloppine

3 pounds veal steak, ¼ to ⅓ inch thick
½ cup enriched flour
1 teaspoon salt
Dash pepper
2 teaspoons paprika
3 tablespoons fat

• • •

1 6-ounce can (1⅓ cups) broiled
    sliced mushrooms
1 bouillon cube

• • •

1 8-ounce can (1 cup) seasoned
    tomato sauce
¼ cup chopped green pepper

• • •

1 8-ounce package green noodles
    (tagliatelle verdi)

Pound the meat thoroughly with meat pounder. Cut in serving pieces. Combine flour and seasonings; coat meat in mixture. Brown in hot fat. Place in 13x9x2-inch baking dish.

Drain mushrooms, reserving liquid. Add water to mushroom liquid to make 1 cup; heat to boiling. Dissolve bouillon cube in the hot liquid and pour over meat.

Bake in moderate oven (350°) 30 minutes. Combine tomato sauce, green pepper, and mushrooms; pour over the meat and continue baking for 15 minutes more.

Meanwhile, cook noodles until tender in boiling salted water; drain. Baste meat with the sauce just before serving. Sprinkle with Parmesan cheese. Serve with hot buttered noodles. Makes 8 to 9 servings.

Veal Stew with Fluffy Dumplings

1 pound veal stew meat, in 1-inch cubes
3 tablespoons fat
2¼ cups hot water
½ cup diced potatoes
½ cup diced carrots
¼ cup chopped celery
¼ cup chopped onion
1 bay leaf
1 teaspoon Worcestershire sauce
¾ teaspoon salt
Dash pepper

• • •

1 recipe Fluffy Dumplings
1 8-ounce can (1 cup) seasoned
    tomato sauce
½ cup fresh, frozen, or canned peas

Roll meat in flour; brown slowly in hot fat. Add hot water; cover and simmer (don't boil) 1 hour. Add potatoes, carrots, celery, onion, bay leaf, Worcestershire sauce, salt, and pepper. Continue cooking 15 to 20 minutes or till meat and vegetables are tender.

Meanwhile, make Fluffy Dumplings.

Add tomato sauce and peas to stew; bring to boiling. Drop dumpling mixture from tablespoon atop bubbling stew. Cover tightly. Reduce heat (don't lift cover), and simmer 12 to 15 minutes longer.

Makes 4 to 5 servings.

Fluffy Dumplings

1 cup sifted enriched flour
2 teaspoons baking powder
¾ teaspoon salt

• • •

½ cup milk
2 tablespoons salad oil or melted
    shortening

Sift together flour, baking powder, and salt. Combine milk and salad oil or shortening; add to dry ingredients, stirring just till flour is moistened.

Cook Dumplings atop hot stew.

For Barbecued Veal, brown cubes of meat on all sides—slowly, but thoroughly. Meanwhile combine ingredients for the sauce; pour over meat. Cover skillet and simmer till fork-tender and delicious.

Barbecued Veal with Rice

Zippy cubes of Barbecued Veal circle mound of fluffy rice—extra-good meal at piggy-bank cost. Long, slow cooking is the secret for best flavor.

Barbecued Veal with Rice

3 pounds boneless breast of veal cut in
   2-inch cubes
2 tablespoons fat
1 8-ounce can (1 cup)
   seasoned tomato sauce
½ cup catsup
½ cup water
1 medium onion, sliced
½ cup chopped celery
2 tablespoons brown sugar
2 tablespoons prepared mustard
1 tablespoon Worcestershire sauce
Hot cooked rice

BETTER HOMES AND GARDENS
$ ECONOMY RECIPE $

Brown veal slowly on all sides in hot fat; season with salt and pepper. Combine remaining ingredients except rice, and pour over meat. Cover and simmer* (don't boil) till tender, about 2 hours, removing cover last 20 minutes. Spoon off excess fat. Mound hot rice in center of platter; circle with the meat; ladle the sauce over meat and rice. Makes 6 servings.

   *Or cover and bake in moderate oven (350°) 2 hours or till tender.

Veal Parmesan

¼ cup enriched flour
1 teaspoon salt
½ teaspoon garlic salt
½ teaspoon paprika
Dash pepper
4 veal loin chops, ¾ inch thick
½ cup fine dry bread crumbs
¼ cup grated Parmesan cheese
1 beaten egg
2 tablespoons olive or salad oil
4 thin slices Mozzarella cheese
1 pound (about 12) tiny new potatoes,
   scraped
1 8-ounce can (1 cup) seasoned tomato
   sauce
1½ tablespoons crushed oregano

Combine flour and seasonings; coat chops. Mix crumbs and Parmesan cheese. Dip chops in egg, then in crumb mixture. Brown slowly in hot oil. Place a slice of Mozzarella cheese atop each chop; arrange potatoes around meat. Pour tomato sauce over; sprinkle with oregano. Cover; simmer 50 minutes or till meat and potatoes are done. Makes 4 servings.

Variety meats–a good choice,

Beefsteak and Kidney Pie

1 small beef kidney

. . .

1 pound round steak
1 medium onion, sliced
3 cups hot water
⅓ cup enriched flour
¼ cup cold water
Salt and pepper to taste
1 stick packaged pastry mix

Soak kidney 1 hour in lukewarm salt water (1 tablespoon salt to 4 cups water). Drain. Remove skin and tubes; cover with cold water; bring to a boil and simmer 20 minutes. Drain.

Cut kidney and steak in 1-inch pieces; roll in flour and brown in a little hot fat. Add onion when meat is partially browned. Add hot water; cover; simmer until tender, about 30 minutes. Thicken with flour blended with cold water. Season. Place in greased 1-quart baking dish.

Prepare 1 stick pastry mix according to package directions. Roll pastry ½ inch larger than casserole. Place pastry over meat mixture; slit top; turn under pastry edge, flute. Bake in very hot oven (450°) 15 minutes. Makes 4 servings.

Pepperpot Soup

½ pound honeycomb tripe
¼ cup chopped celery
½ cup chopped green pepper
½ cup chopped onion
¼ cup butter
1 tablespoon enriched flour
3 cups chicken stock
1 tablespoon celery salt
1 teaspoon pepper
½ cup light cream

Let tripe stand in cold water 4 hours; scrub. Simmer in salted water 3 hours. Drain and dice finely.

Cook celery, green pepper, and onion in 2 tablespoons butter till onion is tender but not brown. Blend in flour; gradually add chicken stock and cook and stir till thick. Add tripe, seasonings. Cover and simmer 1 hour. To serve, add cream and remaining butter. Makes 4 servings.

Kidney Kabobs

Remove outer membrane from lamb or veal kidney. Cut in quarters. Use scissors to snip out white veins and fat. Thread pieces on metal skewers, alternating with 2-inch bacon strips. Add mushroom caps or cherry tomatoes, if desired. Brush generously with melted butter. Broil 3 inches from heat 7 minutes. Turn and broil 5 to 7 minutes more or till well browned.

Ham and Sweetbread Roll-ups

1 tablespoon vinegar
1 pound fresh or frozen sweetbreads

. . .

6 thin slices boiled ham
1 can condensed cream of chicken soup
2 tablespoons chopped parsley
¼ cup grated Parmesan cheese

Combine 1 quart lightly salted water and vinegar. Add sweetbreads and simmer (don't boil) 20 minutes or till tender. Drain; remove membranes.

Spread each ham slice with 1 tablespoon soup; sprinkle with parsley. Center sweetbreads on ham slices; roll up each and fasten with toothpicks.

Place in shallow baking dish. Sprinkle with cheese. Bake in hot oven (400°) 20 minutes or till heated through. Makes 6 servings. Pass *Sour-cream Sauce:* Add ½ teaspoon monosodium glutamate to remaining soup; heat and stir. Blend in 1 cup dairy sour cream; heat through and serve.

Spiced Tongue

2 veal or baby-beef tongues
Hot water
3 whole black peppers
6 whole cloves
2 teaspoons salt
2 bay leaves
1 tablespoon vinegar

Cover tongues with hot water; simmer 1 hour. Add peppers, cloves, salt, bay leaves, and vinegar. Cover and simmer till tender, about 2 hours. Cool. Remove skin and trim roots. Slice in thin crosswise slices.

a change of pace

Stuffed Veal Hearts

2 veal hearts
2 tablespoons chopped onion
3 tablespoons fat
1½ cups cracker crumbs
¾ teaspoon salt
¼ teaspoon pepper
¼ teaspoon celery salt
¼ cup water

. . .

Enriched flour
1 can condensed consomme
2 whole cloves
3 whole black peppers
1 bay leaf

Clean hearts, removing arteries and veins; make pocket for stuffing.

Lightly brown onion in hot fat; add cracker crumbs and seasonings; mix well. Add water. Stuff hearts with this mixture; close opening and fasten with skewers.

Roll in flour. Brown in hot fat; add remaining ingredients. Cover tightly and cook slowly 1½ hours. Makes 6 servings.

Old-time Oxtail Stew

2 pounds oxtail, cut in 1½-inch lengths
1 medium onion, sliced
1 1-pound can (2 cups) tomatoes
1 can condensed beef broth
1½ teaspoons salt
¼ teaspoon pepper
8 small whole onions
4 potatoes, halved
4 carrots, halved

Roll meat in flour; brown in small amount hot fat in Dutch oven. Add 2 cups hot water, the sliced onion, tomatoes, broth, and seasonings. Cover; simmer 2½ hours or till meat is just tender. Add vegetables; cover and simmer 30 to 45 minutes or till done. Skim off excess fat. Makes 4 to 6 servings.

Brains

Cover with cold water; add 2 tablespoons vinegar. Soak 30 minutes. Drain. Remove loose membranes. Simmer in salted water 20 to 30 minutes. Drain; chill in cold water. Drain. Season; dip into beaten egg, then into cracker crumbs. Fry in hot fat.

Or dice cooked, chilled brains; add to white sauce with peas. Or scramble with eggs.

Cook tongue at a lazy bubble, serve with a spicy sauce

Tongue with Gingersnap Sauce

1 2- to 4-pound smoked beef tongue
1 onion, sliced
1 teaspoon cloves
1 teaspoon whole black peppers
4 bay leaves

. . .

1 recipe Gingersnap Sauce

Cover meat with water. Add onion and spices. Cover and simmer till tender, allowing 1 hour per pound. Remove meat; strain and reserve liquid. Cut off bones and gristle from large end; slit skin on underside from large end to tip; peel off. Slice meat on a slant. Makes about 4 servings per pound. Serve with hot Gingersnap Sauce.

Gingersnap Sauce: Crush 5 gingersnaps; combine with ⅓ cup brown sugar, ⅓ cup seedless raisins, ¼ cup vinegar, 1 cup reserved liquid. Cook and stir till smooth.

Pep up your luncheon or evening meal with smoked tongue and Gingersnap Sauce. The sauce accents the distinctive tongue flavor. What's more, the fixing's minimum.

Five good ways to serve liver

Here are points aplenty why you should put liver on your shopping list more often.

Liver is loaded with minerals and vitamins. It's the top source of iron and vitamin A, rich in the B vitamins, too.

You don't have to let your purse be your guide in buying liver. Most tender and most expensive are calf, veal, and lamb liver. But baby-beef liver costs less and is tender enough to broil or fry. Pork and beef liver are real bargains. Try them braised for delicious flavor, tenderness.

When it comes to variety of preparation, it's hard to beat liver. Broil, pan-fry, braise, or French-fry liver. Grind it for liver loaf or patties. Serve it with onions, bacon, or tomatoes. Try these easy recipes, and your family will ask for liver again—soon!

Braise

Remove membrane from ½-inch slices of beef or pork liver. Snip out veins with scissors.

Dip liver in flour. Season with salt and pepper. Brown quickly on both sides in small amount of hot fat. Reduce heat. Add ½ cup bouillon (or 1 bouillon cube dissolved in ½ cup hot water). Cover skillet. Cook till tender, about 20 minutes.

Pan-fry

You'll go for the crusty coating of liver fixed this way.

Remove membrane and veins from slices of liver—veal, calf, baby beef, or lamb. Dip in well-seasoned flour. Brown quickly in hot fat; turn and brown other side *just until done*—don't overcook. Serve piping hot with fried onions or bacon.

French-fry

Out of the deep-fat fryer it comes— →
tender strips of liver with crisp jackets.
Delicious—an especially tasty way to
cook pork liver.

Remove membrane from liver and
snip out veins with kitchen scissors.
Cut liver in ½-inch strips. Marinate in
French dressing ½ hour; drain. Dip in
beaten egg, roll in cracker crumbs.
(Tongs make this job easy.) Fry liver
in deep hot fat (360°) till browned.
Drain on paper towels.

Broil

A favorite with the men! It takes
only 6 minutes to broil liver just right.

Remove membrane and veins from
slices of liver—veal, calf, baby beef, or
lamb. Place on cold broiler pan; brush
with butter or French dressing. Broil 3
inches from heat 3 minutes; turn; top
with bacon slices to keep moist. Broil
3 to 4 minutes or till bacon is done.

↓

Grind for loaf

Liver Loaf

1 pound beef liver
1 medium onion, chopped
½ pound pork sausage
1 cup dry bread crumbs
1 teaspoon Worcestershire sauce
1 tablespoon lemon juice
1 teaspoon salt
1 teaspoon celery salt
Dash pepper
2 beaten eggs
½ cup stock
4 slices bacon

Cover liver with hot water; simmer 5 minutes. Drain liquid and reserve for stock.

Put liver and onion through food chopper,
using medium blade. Add remaining ingredients, except bacon.

Form in loaf in 10x5x3-inch loaf pan. Top
with bacon slices. Bake in moderate oven
(350°) 45 minutes. Makes 6 to 8 servings.

For good stick-to-the-ribs fare, you can't beat ground meat

Nothing everyday about this trio of meat loaves. Each one is moist, temptingly seasoned

Glazed Ham-loaf Ring

1½ pounds ground ham
1¼ pounds ground fresh pork
1½ cups soft bread crumbs
½ cup chopped onion
2 beaten eggs
½ cup milk
1 recipe Sweet-sour Glaze
1 recipe Mustard Sauce

Thoroughly combine meats, crumbs, onion, eggs, and milk. Press mixture into lightly oiled 6½-cup ring mold; invert on shallow baking pan, remove ring mold. Bake in moderate oven (350°) 1¼ *hours in all.*

At the end of 45 minutes' baking time, brush loaf with *Sweet-sour Glaze:* Blend ½ cup brown sugar and 1 tablespoon prepared mustard; stir in 2 tablespoons vinegar, 1 tablespoon water. Continue baking loaf till done, basting 3 or 4 times. Serve with Mustard Sauce. Makes 10 to 12 servings.

Mustard Sauce: In jar, mix ½ cup dry mustard and ½ cup vinegar; cover, let stand overnight. In top of double boiler, beat 1 egg; stir in ⅓ cup sugar, dash salt, and mustard mixture. Cook over *hot (not boiling)* water, stirring constantly, till mixture thickens slightly and coats spoon. Cool. To serve, add mayonnaise—about half and half.

Tender, tasty meat loaves

Top, Twin Meat Loaves—chili-sauce topper adds color and tang; left corner, Glazed Ham-loaf Ring; on wood platter, Favorite Beef Loaf along with herbed tomatoes.

Twin Meat Loaves

1 pound ground beef
½ pound ground pork
½ pound ground veal
⅓ cup chopped onion
3 tablespoons finely chopped celery
Seasonings (below)
4 slices soft bread, cubed
1 cup warm milk
2 eggs
Chili Topper

Thoroughly mix beef, pork, and veal. Add chopped onion and celery. Stir in seasonings: 2 teaspoons salt, ½ teaspoon poultry seasoning or sage, ¼ teaspoon dry mustard, ¼ teaspoon pepper, and 1 tablespoon Worcestershire sauce.

Soak cubed bread in milk; add eggs; beat with rotary beater. Combine meat and egg mixtures. Form in 2 loaves. *Chili Topper:* Roll loaves in ½ cup fine dry bread crumbs. Place in greased shallow baking pan. Spread ¼ cup chili sauce over each loaf. Pour ½ cup boiling water around loaves. Bake in moderate oven (350°) 1 hour. Drizzle chili sauce over tops. Makes 8 to 10 servings.

Favorite Beef Loaf

⅔ cup fine cracker crumbs
1 cup milk
1½ pounds ground beef
2 beaten eggs
½ cup chopped onion
1 teaspoon salt
1 teaspoon monosodium glutamate
½ to ¾ teaspoon ground sage
　 or poultry seasoning
Dash pepper

Soak cracker crumbs in milk; add meat, eggs, onion, and seasonings; mix well. Shape in loaf in shallow baking pan, or lightly pack into 8½x4½x2½-inch loaf pan. Bake at 350° 45 to 50 minutes. Garnish with green pepper and onion rings. Makes 8 servings.

Here's how to turn out juicy, just-right burgers

● Look for bright red color. If you have beef ground to order, choose round steak, chuck, flank, sirloin tip. If meat is lean, have 2 or 3 ounces suet ground with each pound. You'll taste the difference—burgers will be juicier.

● Medium- or coarsely ground meat gives a nice light burger—best kind!

● Give ground meat velvet-glove treatment. Gentle handling makes for tender burgers. Same goes for heat—overcooking dries meat out, makes it a real toughy.

● Like burgers to be all the same size? Use a ⅓- or ½-cup measure as a guide for amount of meat per patty.

● For each pound of ground beef, use ½ teaspoon monosodium glutamate.

● When you're making burgers for the crowd, stack them up—all set to broil. Put waxed paper between each layer.

● When broiling or skillet-cooking, just turn meat once.

● Burgers need to wait a few minutes after cooking? Here's a way to keep them piping hot, extra juicy. While burgers broil, heat equal amount of butter or margarine and Worcestershire sauce—enough to coat burgers. When patties are done to your liking, transfer to sauce in the hot skillet, turning once.

Hamburgers

> ½ cup chopped onion, optional
> Fat
> 1 pound ground beef
> 1 teaspoon salt
> Dash pepper

Cook onion in small amount hot fat till tender, but not brown. Combine onion, meat, seasonings. Mix thoroughly. Form balls, using ½- or ⅓-cup measure. Pat in thick burgers or roll thin patties between squares of waxed paper. Fry till done to your liking. Or broil 3 inches from heat about 6 minutes; turn, broil about 6 minutes more. Makes 4 to 6 servings.

You may like additional seasonings—Worchestershire sauce, smoked salt, barbecue sauce, catsup, or mustard.

Smoky Cheeseburgers

Prepare 6 meat patties as above. While burgers cook, combine 1 5-ounce jar smoky cheese spread, 1 tablespoon pickle relish, and 2 teaspoons prepared mustard; spread on top half of 6 split hamburger buns. Broil 1 to 2 minutes, or till cheese bubbles and buns toast. Put buns together with meat patty in each. Makes 6 servings.

Skilletburgers

Sauce is good in toasted buns—or spoon, rabbit-style, over bun halves—

> 1 pound ground beef
> 1 tablespoon fat
> 1½ cups chopped onion
> 1½ cups chopped celery
> 1 8-ounce can (1 cup) seasoned tomato sauce
> 1 can condensed tomato soup
> Few drops Tabasco sauce
> 1 teaspoon salt
> ½ teaspoon monosodium glutamate
> ¼ teaspoon chili powder
> Dash pepper
> 5 or 6 hamburger buns, split and toasted

Brown meat in hot fat. Add onion and celery; cook till tender but not brown. Add tomato sauce, soup, and seasonings.

Simmer uncovered about 20 minutes or until the consistency you like. Spoon mixture into toasted buns. Makes 5 or 6 servings.

Burger Topping

Whip butter (use mixer or wooden spoon) and add crumbled blue cheese to taste. Spoon generous blob on burgers just before whisking from broiler to platter.

Special Hamburgers

1 pound ground beef
2 tablespoons finely chopped green
    pepper
¼ cup chopped onion
3 tablespoons catsup
1 tablespoon horseradish
1 teaspoon salt
½ teaspoon dry mustard

Combine ingredients and mix well. Form in patties. Broil, or place in greased shallow baking dish and bake in moderate oven (375°) 30 minutes. Makes 4 to 6.

Cheeseburger Towers

2 pounds ground beef
¼ cup finely chopped onion
1 tablespoon prepared mustard
1 tablespoon Worcestershire sauce
1½ teaspoons prepared horseradish
Salt and pepper
6 slices process American cheese
6 hamburger buns, split and toasted

Combine meat, onion, and seasonings. Shape in 12 patties a little less than ½ inch thick. Cook in lightly greased skillet about 6 minutes, turning once. With cooky cutter, cut a 2-inch round from center of each cheese slice. Place half the meat patties in toasted buns; add cheese slice, filling the hole in cheese with catsup, mustard, or barbecue, hamburger, or hot-dog relish. Top with remaining meat patties and cheese rounds. Makes 6.

Cheese-stuffed Hamburger Roll

¼ cup chopped onion
3 cups toasted bread cubes
1½ pounds ground beef
1 egg
1 teaspoon salt
¼ teaspoon pepper
¼ teaspoon sage
1¼ cups grated sharp process cheese

Simmer onion in ⅓ cup boiling water 5 minutes; pour over bread. Combine meat, egg, seasonings; pat out in 14x8-inch rectangle on waxed paper. Spread bread mixture over; sprinkle 1 cup of the cheese atop. Roll. Place in 8½x4½x2½-inch loaf pan. Bake in moderate oven (350°) 70 minutes. Sprinkle remaining cheese over; bake 2 minutes longer. Makes 4 to 6 servings.

Betterburgers are plump, juicy, tender—the best you've ever tasted! The secrets: Shape with a gentle touch; cook in "salted" skillet; serve when just done

To keep patties light, try shaping them this no-pack way. Place whole package of hamburger on original wrapping or waxed paper. Using fingertips, gently form meat into a roll about 3 inches thick. Cut roll into ½- to ¾-inch slices. Round edges of patties if you like.

Or, roll meat between big sheets of waxed paper to ½ inch; cut with jumbo cooky cutter.

Heat skillet sizzling hot. Shake salt into empty skillet—the same amount as if you were salting burgers, ½ to 1 teaspoon. Put burgers in pan; sear on one side only—about 1 minute.

Lower heat, cook a few minutes. Turn burgers, cook 2 or 3 minutes on second side, or till done to your liking. Serve on toasted garlic bread. (One pound hamburger makes 4 burgers.)

Dinner on the double—
Lamb-patty broiler meal

Easy—it all broils together. In less than 30 minutes, every-thing is ready for the table—juicy lamb patties, butter-browned potatoes, hot peaches filled with mint jelly.

Lamb-patty Broiler Dinner

Mix 1 pound ground lamb with 1 teaspoon salt, dash each monosodium glutamate and thyme or marjoram, and ¼ cup milk. Shape lightly in 4 oval patties. Score with handle of wooden spoon or spatula.

Arrange meal on broiler pan—patties; drained, canned peach halves; drained, canned potatoes in foilware pan (or make your own). Drizzle melted butter over pota-toes. Broil 4 to 5 inches from heat 12 min-utes. Turn patties. Brush potatoes again with melted butter. Sprinkle with salt, pep-per, and paprika. Broil 5 minutes. Fill peach centers with mint jelly. Top each patty with bacon slice. Broil about 5 minutes more, or till patties are done.

Veal Patties

1½ pounds ground veal
¼ cup melted fat
½ teaspoon lemon juice
½ teaspoon paprika
¼ teaspoon nutmeg
Salt and pepper
1 beaten egg
2 tablespoons water
1 cup dry bread crumbs

Combine meat, fat, lemon juice, and sea-sonings; form patties. Mix egg with water. Dip patties into egg mixture, then into bread crumbs. Brown in hot fat. Cook 15 minutes. If desired, serve with gravy seasoned with lemon juice and a dash of nutmeg. Makes 6 to 8 servings.

Meat Balls in Mushroom Sauce

1 pound ground beef
½ pound ground pork
2 slightly beaten eggs
⅔ cup grated Parmesan cheese
½ teaspoon crushed oregano
¼ teaspoon thyme
Dash pepper
1 can condensed cream of mushroom
    soup

Mix meats, eggs, cheese, and seasonings; shape in about thirty 1½-inch balls; brown *slowly* on all sides in a little hot fat, about 20 minutes. Drain off excess fat. Pour in soup; add ⅔ cup water slowly, stirring to blend. Simmer uncovered 20 to 25 minutes, stirring occasionally. Sprinkle with chopped parsley before serving. Makes 6 servings.

Swedish Meat Balls

¼ cup chopped onion
1 tablespoon butter or margarine
½ pound ground beef
½ pound ground veal
¾ teaspoon salt
Dash white pepper
2 tablespoons enriched flour
1 egg
¼ cup light cream
1 can condensed consomme

Cook onion in butter till tender but not brown. Combine meats and seasonings; *beat thoroughly*. Beat in flour; then egg. Gradually beat in cream. Add onion. (This mixture should be light and fluffy.) Form mixture in 1-inch balls and lightly brown in a little additional butter, shaking skillet to turn balls. Remove excess fat. Add consomme; cook uncovered 12 to 15 minutes. If desired, thicken gravy. Makes 2 dozen.

Ham Patties with Sour Cream

2 cups ground cooked ham
½ cup soft bread crumbs
¼ cup chopped green onion
⅓ cup milk
1 slightly beaten egg
Dash pepper
1 cup dairy sour cream

Combine all ingredients except sour cream. Shape mixture in 6 small or 4 large patties. Brown slowly on both sides in a small amount of hot fat. Heat sour cream just until hot and serve with patties. Trim with chopped onion tops. Makes 3 or 4 servings.

Meat Balls Supreme

Best-ever meat balls!—

3 slices bread
¾ cup hot milk
1 beaten egg
¾ pound ground beef
¼ pound ground pork
3 tablespoons grated onion
3 tablespoons chopped parsley
Salt
Pepper
2 tablespoons fat
. . .
2 cups tomato juice
1 teaspoon kitchen bouquet
1 cup hot water
½ cup chopped carrots
½ cup chopped celery
. . .
1 cup canned peas

Soften bread in milk; add egg. Mix meats; add onion, parsley, and salt and pepper. Combine mixtures; form in balls; roll in flour; brown in hot fat.

Add tomato juice and kitchen bouquet; simmer 10 minutes; add water, carrots, and celery. Cover; simmer 30 minutes. Add peas; continue cooking till peas heat through. Makes 6 servings.

Meat Balls Stroganoff

Here's a dish to make you famous. Success secret—the sour-cream mushroom sauce—

1 cup medium cracker crumbs
1 teaspoon salt
Dash pepper
Dash thyme *or* oregano
¾ cup milk
2 eggs
1 pound ground beef
¾ pound ground pork
2 tablespoons butter or margarine
1 beef bouillon cube
½ cup boiling water
. . .
1 6-ounce can (1⅓ cups) broiled
    sliced mushrooms, drained
1 cup dairy sour cream

Combine crumbs, salt, pepper, thyme or oregano, milk, and eggs. Add meats; mix well. Form meat mixture in balls (1½ inches across); brown slowly on all sides in hot fat. Combine bouillon cube and water; pour over meat. Cook covered over low heat for 30 minutes. Add mushrooms and sour cream; heat just to boiling. Serves 6 to 8.

Ham Croquettes

3 tablespoons butter or margarine
⅓ cup sifted enriched flour
½ teaspoon salt
1 cup milk
2 cups coarsely ground cooked ham
1 tablespoon finely chopped onion
2 tablespoons prepared mustard
1 beaten egg
½ cup fine cracker crumbs

Melt butter, blend in flour. Add salt and milk and cook over low heat until thick, stirring constantly. Cool. Add ham, onion, and mustard. Chill.

Shape in croquettes. Dip in egg, then in crumbs. Let stand a few minutes. Fry in deep, hot fat (375°) 7 to 8 minutes, or until brown. Drain on paper towels. Makes 12 croquettes, or 6 servings.

Serve with *Creamy Egg Sauce:* Melt 2 tablespoons butter or margarine; blend in 2 tablespoons enriched flour. Slowly stir in 1 cup milk; cook and stir till thick. Add ¼ teaspoon salt, dash pepper, and 2 chopped hard-cooked eggs. Sprinkle with sieved hard-cooked egg yolk.

Chili Con Carne

1½ cups red chili beans or 1 No. 2 can
  (2½ cups) kidney beans
1 large onion, sliced
1 green pepper, chopped
1 pound ground beef
3 tablespoons fat
2 1-pound cans (4 cups) tomatoes
1 to 1½ tablespoons chili powder
1½ teaspoons salt
3 whole cloves
1 bay leaf
Dash paprika
Dash cayenne pepper

Soak chili beans overnight. Cook in boiling, salted water until tender. Drain.

Brown onion, green pepper, and meat in hot fat. Add tomatoes and seasonings. Simmer 2 hours adding water if necessary. Add beans; heat thoroughly. Makes 6 servings.

20-minute Italian Spaghetti

1 pound ground beef
4 or 5 medium onions, sliced
3 or 4 cloves garlic, minced
2 tablespoons salad oil
2 cups water
2 6-ounce cans (1⅓ cups) tomato paste
1 8-ounce can (1 cup) tomato sauce
1 tablespoon chili powder
1 teaspoon salt
½ teaspoon cayenne pepper
Dash pepper

Combine all ingredients in pressure pan. Adjust cover. Exhaust air from cooker. Cook at 15 pounds pressure 20 minutes.

Reduce pressure quickly. Serve the meat sauce over cooked spaghetti (one 8-ounce package long spaghetti). Top with grated Parmesan cheese. Makes 6 servings.

Ham Croquettes

A tasty comeback for Sunday's ham. You can shape these croquettes early and chill. Then French-fry a little before mealtime. Cap croquettes with Creamy Egg Sauce, sprinkle with sieved hard-cooked egg yolk. Serve with nut-filled broiled peaches.

Meat Balls and Spaghetti. Can't beat a good spaghetti supper, especially with this sauce.

Meat Balls and Spaghetti

¾ cup chopped onion
3 tablespoons olive or salad oil
2 1-pound cans (4 cups) tomatoes
2 6-ounce cans (1⅓ cups) tomato paste
1 tablespoon sugar
1½ teaspoons salt
½ teaspoon pepper
1 bay leaf
1½ teaspoons crushed oregano
4 slices dry bread
1 pound ground beef
2 eggs
½ cup grated Romano cheese
2 tablespoons chopped parsley
1 clove garlic, minced
1 teaspoon crushed oregano
1 teaspoon salt

Cook chopped onion in hot oil until tender. Add next seven ingredients and 1 cup water. Simmer 30 minutes; remove bay leaf.

Soak bread in water 2 or 3 minutes; squeeze out moisture. Mix bread with remaining ingredients. Shape in about 20 balls. Brown in hot oil. Add to sauce, cook 30 minutes. Serve over spaghetti. Serves 6.

Italian Spaghetti Sauce

½ cup onion slices
2 tablespoons olive or salad oil
1 pound ground beef
2 cloves garlic, minced
2 1-pound cans (4 cups) tomatoes
2 8-ounce cans (2 cups) seasoned
   tomato sauce
1 cup water
1 3-ounce can (⅔ cup) broiled
   sliced mushrooms
¼ cup chopped parsley
1½ teaspoons oregano or sage
1 teaspoon salt
½ teaspoon monosodium glutamate
¼ teaspoon thyme
1 bay leaf
Long spaghetti, cooked
Grated Parmesan or Romano cheese

Cook onion in hot oil till golden. Add meat and garlic; brown lightly. Add remaining ingredients; simmer uncovered 2 to 2½ hours or till thick. Remove bay leaf.

Serve sauce on hot cooked spaghetti. Pass bowl of grated Parmesan or Romano cheese for folks to help themselves. Makes 6 servings.

For quick and easy meals – franks

Time was when frankfurters were only picnic or family fare. Now they are socially acceptable at the best tables. Choose the short stouts or long skinnies—call them hot dogs, red hots, or franks. They're all delicious— in toasted buns or tangy sauce

"Frank" Fries are heaped high in the center bowl. They're fast as skat, look smart, taste good. Use the serving tongs to tuck one in a hot buttered bun from basket.

Turn the Susan and help yourself to pickle relish, radishes, onion and cucumber rounds, carrot strips, gherkins, tomato slices, and sticks of crisp green pepper.

Kettle-cooked Wieners

Place franks in boiling water; cover and reduce heat; simmer (don't boil) 5 to 8 minutes. Lift out with tongs.

"Frank" Fries

Score frankfurters, making shallow (¼-inch) diagonal cuts 1 inch apart. Brown in skillet in 1 tablespoon hot fat 3 to 5 minutes. Be careful not to overbrown.

Wiener Doubles

16 frankfurters
2 tablespoons prepared mustard
Sharp process American cheese
16 bacon strips

Slit franks lengthwise, not quite through. Spread cut surfaces with mustard and insert strip of cheese in each slit. For each serving, place 2 franks side by side. Wrap 2 strips of bacon around each bundle in spiral fashion; fasten ends with toothpicks. Place franks cheese-side down on broiler rack, 3 to 4 inches from heat. Broil about 5 minutes or till bacon on top side is done. Turn and broil 3 to 5 minutes longer. Serve with halved coney buns, toasted and buttered. Makes 8 servings.

To cook over hot coals, broil cheese-side down till bacon is done on bottom. Turn cheese-side up, and broil till done.

Barbecued Frankfurters

¼ cup chopped onion
1 cup catsup
½ cup water
½ cup chopped celery
¼ cup lemon juice
2 tablespoons brown sugar
3 tablespoons Worcestershire sauce
2 tablespoons vinegar
1 tablespoon prepared mustard
½ teaspoon salt
Dash pepper
Dash cayenne

• • •

1½ pounds (about 12) frankfurters

Cook onion in hot fat till tender. Combine remaining ingredients (except frankfurters) and add to onion. Cover and simmer 20 minutes. Prick frankfurters; add to sauce. Cover, simmer 15 minutes. Makes 6 servings.

Wiener Heights

8 onion slices
8 ½-inch slices peeled tomato
1 small green pepper, cut in strips
½ cup thin bias-cut celery slices
8 frankfurters
1 cup shredded sharp process American cheese

Place onion slices in greased skillet; top each with tomato. Season with salt, pepper. Place 2 or 3 green-pepper strips and some celery slices on each tomato. Halve frankfurters lengthwise, then crosswise; place 2 pieces, cut side up, on each tower; top with 2 more. Cover and heat slowly 10 to 15 minutes or till hot and vegetables are crisp-done. Sprinkle with cheese, paprika. Serve with hot French Bread. Makes 4 servings.

Coney Islands

Place 1½ pounds (about 12) franks in boiling water; reduce heat and simmer (don't boil) 5 to 8 minutes. Set everything out, help-yourself style; let folks pop franks in heated coney buns, smear on prepared mustard, spoon on chopped onion, then hot Coney Sauce. Makes 12 Coneys.

Coney Sauce

½ pound ground beef
¼ cup water
¼ cup chopped onion
1 clove garlic, minced
1 8-ounce can (1 cup) seasoned tomato sauce
½ to ¾ teaspoon chili powder
½ teaspoon monosodium glutamate
½ teaspoon salt

Brown ground beef slowly but thoroughly, breaking with a fork till fine. Add remaining ingredients; simmer uncovered 10 minutes. Makes sauce for 12 Coneys.

Jiffy Cheesefurters

Split 1 pound (8 to 10) frankfurters lengthwise, cutting only about ¾ the way through. Place in shallow baking dish. Spread cut surfaces with one 6-ounce roll process cheese food—pepper, garlic, smoky, or bacon flavor. Crush one 3-ounce package corn chips (about 1 cup). Sprinkle generously over cheese. Bake in moderate oven (350°) 15 minutes, until heated through.

Frank 'n Corn Crown

½ cup chopped green pepper
¼ cup chopped onion
¼ cup butter or margarine
4 cups soft bread crumbs
2 1-pound cans (4 cups) cream-style
    corn
2 beaten eggs
1 teaspoon salt
½ cup dry bread crumbs
2 tablespoons butter, melted
1½ pounds frankfurters (about 12),
    cut in half crosswise

Cook green pepper and onion in ¼ cup butter till onion is golden but not brown. Add soft bread crumbs, corn, eggs, and salt; mix lightly. Combine dry bread crumbs, 2 tablespoons melted butter; set aside. Place corn mixture in 8x1½-inch round baking dish, mounding in center; sprinkle top with buttered crumbs. Bake uncovered in moderate oven (350°) 25 minutes; stand frankfurters cut end down in a crown around edge of stuffing, and continue baking 15 minutes longer. Makes 6 to 8 servings.

Red Hots en Kabob

½ pound (4 to 5) frankfurters, cut
    in 1-inch chunks
. . .
½ cup soy sauce
⅓ cup catsup
¼ cup salad oil
¼ cup vinegar
1 teaspoon thyme
1 teaspoon prepared mustard
. . .
16 small cooked or canned onions
16 canned pineapple chunks, drained
2 green peppers, cut in 1-inch squares
8 slices bacon, cut in half crosswise
2 large, firm tomatoes, cut in eighths
8 9- or 10-inch skewers

With sharp knife, score cut ends of frankfurter pieces. Combine next 6 ingredients for marinade; pour over franks, onions, pineapple, and green pepper and chill 3 hours or overnight.

Wrap a bacon piece around each pineapple chunk. Alternate the chunks of frankfurter, vegetables, and bacon-wrapped pineapple on skewers. Broil 3 to 4 inches from heat 5 to 7 minutes on first side; turn and broil 3 to 4 minutes longer or till bacon is done. While cooking, brush occasionally with the marinade. Makes 4 or 5 servings.

Deviled Hot Dogs

½ cup finely chopped onion
2 tablespoons chopped green pepper
2 tablespoons salad oil
. . .
1 pound (8 to 10) frankfurters
¾ cup catsup
2 tablespoons brown sugar
2 tablespoons prepared mustard
1 tablespoon Worcestershire sauce
1 teaspoon salt

Cook onion and green pepper in hot oil till tender but not brown. Score frankfurters diagonally; add with remaining ingredients to onion mixture; cover and simmer 5 to 8 minutes. Makes 4 or 5 servings.

Franks a la foil

2 cups finely chopped frankfurters
    (about 6 franks)
⅓ cup shredded sharp process
    American cheese
2 hard-cooked eggs, chopped
3 tablespoons chili sauce
2 tablespoons pickle relish
1 teaspoon prepared mustard
½ to ¾ teaspoon garlic salt
. . .
6 coney buns, split

Combine all ingredients except buns. Partially hollow out soft centers of buns; fill with frankfurter mixture and close.

Wrap each bun in foil, sealing securely. Place on baking sheet; bake in hot oven (400°) 12 to 15 minutes. (Or heat on grill over coals.) Makes 6 servings.

Frankfurters Hawaiian

1 8-ounce can (1 cup) seasoned
    tomato sauce
1 9-ounce can (1 cup) pineapple tidbits
½ teaspoon salt
1 tablespoon brown sugar
1 tablespoon vinegar
1 tablespoon prepared mustard
1 tablespoon finely chopped onion or
    1 teaspoon instant minced onion
½ to 1 teaspoon chili powder
. . .
1 pound (8 to 10) frankfurters

In skillet, combine all ingredients except frankfurters. Simmer, uncovered, 5 minutes. Add frankfurters; cover and simmer 5 to 8 minutes longer or till heated through.

Makes 4 or 5 servings.

Franks go fancy—in creole sauce or toasty jackets

Creole Franks skillet-cook in a tomato sauce spiked with pineapple juice and chili powder—sweet *and* sour. Wiener Winks boast blankets of toast, Parmesan cheese, mustard, onion, and stuffed-olive toppers.

Creole Franks

    5 slices bacon, diced
    ½ cup chopped onion
    1 cup unsweetened pineapple
       juice
    ¾ cup catsup
    ⅛ teaspoon chili powder
    1½ pounds (about 12) frankfurters
    ¼ cup chopped green pepper

Cook the bacon but do not crisp. Add chopped onion and cook till tender but not brown. Stir in the unsweetened pineapple juice, catsup, and chili powder.

Score franks diagonally at 1-inch intervals; add to the sauce. Cover and bring to boiling; add chopped green pepper and simmer 8 to 10 minutes. Serve on fluffy hot rice, if desired. Makes 6 servings.

Wiener Winks

    8 frankfurters
    8 thin slices bread, crusts removed
    ½ cup grated Parmesan cheese
    3 tablespoons finely chopped onion
    3 tablespoons prepared mustard
    8 stuffed green olives

Place frankfurters in boiling water; cover, reduce heat, simmer 5 to 8 minutes; drain.

Butter bread. Dip buttered side in cheese. Combine onion and mustard; spread on unbuttered side of bread and place a frankfurter diagonally across each slice. Fasten 2 opposite corners of slice with toothpick. Place bread side down on broiler pan; broil 3 inches from heat 2 or 3 minutes on each side to toast. Perch olives on toothpicks. Makes 8.

Spice your meals with sausage

California Curry Platter

2 hard-cooked eggs
¾ cup golden raisins
2 cups cooked rice
2 tablespoons finely chopped onion
1 tablespoon snipped parsley
¼ teaspoon salt
Dash pepper
3 tablespoons butter or margarine
2 tablespoons cornstarch
1 teaspoon curry powder
1 teaspoon monosodium glutamate
¼ teaspoon salt
3 cups milk
12 slices (or 6 extra-thick slices)
   chopped ham

• • •

Chutney Peaches

Chop hard-cooked eggs, reserving 1 egg yolk to sieve for garnish. Combine the chopped eggs, raisins, rice, onion, parsley, salt, and pepper. Melt butter or margarine; blend in cornstarch, curry powder, monosodium glutamate, and salt. Add milk; cook and stir till mixture thickens and boils. Add *half* the curry sauce to the rice mixture; blend. Spoon rice mixture into large oval or rectangular (13x9x2-inch) baking dish, leaving space at one side to add peaches later. Using 2 slices chopped ham for each roll (or 1 extra-thick slice), place the meat over rice, tucking sides of meat into rice mixture. Pour remaining sauce over rolls. Bake in moderate oven (350°) for 25 minutes. Arrange Chutney Peaches alongside rice. Bake 10 to 15 minutes longer, or till peaches are heated through. Garnish ham rolls with sieved egg yolk. Makes 6 servings.

Baked Chutney Peaches: Drain 6 canned peach halves. Place, cut side up, on cake rack. Brush with melted butter or margarine. Spoon 1 tablespoon chutney into center of each peach half. Place in baking dish with curried chopped ham rolls and rice. Bake in moderate oven (350°) for 10 to 15 minutes or till heated through. Serve hot.

This wonderful taste combination can be served with pork, ham, and other meats.

California Curry Platter is so handsome and good you'll prize it as a company special and still serve it for a family treat. A smooth, mild curry sauce flavor-blends chopped ham, rice, and raisins.

Duo Sausage Pizza offers a pair of sausages. Pepperoni slices ring the outside while Cotto salami cornucopias radiate from the center. Package mix plus extras gives real homemade appeal.

Duo Sausage Pizza

For an even quicker start, use a frozen cheese pizza and top with extras—

- 1 package Cheese Pizza mix
- 2 teaspoons olive oil
- 1 6-ounce package sliced Mozzarella cheese, cut in thirds
- 1 4-ounce package sliced pepperoni

. . .

- 6 slices Cotto salami
- 6 stuffed green olives
- Parsley

Prepare pizza crust according to package directions. Roll or pat out to fit 12- or 14-inch pizza pan. Crimp edges with fork; brush dough with olive oil. Shake on *half* the grated cheese from mix package; cover with pizza sauce; top with circle of overlapping Mozzarella cheese pieces; sprinkle with remaining grated cheese. Place pepperoni slices in a ring around outer edge. Bake in a hot oven (425°) for 15 to 20 minutes or till crust is done.

Roll salami slices in cone shape. Arrange, spoke fashion, in center of pizza, seam side down. Garnish with stuffed green olive in each salami cone and sprig of parsley in center of salami "wheel." Makes 6 servings.

Pat-a-cake Sausage Bake

Tiny sausage patties, no larger than a silver dollar, make this hearty casserole a little different, a little better—

- 1 pound fresh pork sausage

. . .

- 4 ounces (2½ cups) fine noodles
- 2 tablespoons chopped green pepper
- 2 tablespoons chopped canned pimiento
- 1 10½-ounce can condensed cream of chicken soup

. . .

- ⅓ cup buttered cracker crumbs

By rolling a small amount of sausage between hands, form sausage into "marbles" then flatten with fingers into patties the size of a silver dollar. Place small patties in a cold skillet and brown lightly on both sides.

In a large saucepan, cook noodles in boiling *unsalted* water till tender; drain. In a greased 1½-quart casserole, combine the cooked noodles, chopped green pepper, pimiento, soup, and sausage patties. Top casserole with buttered cracker crumbs.

Bake in a moderate oven (350°) for 30 minutes. Makes about 6 servings.

Ready for the table—
canned meats or cold cuts

Chilled-ham Glaze

Measure liquid or jelly from canned ham; add water to make 1½ cups. Add ½ cup brown sugar, ⅓ cup light corn syrup, 1 tablespoon each vinegar and mixed pickling spices; simmer 5 minutes. Strain.

Combine 2 tablespoons each cornstarch and cold water; stir into hot mixture. Cook and stir till clear and slightly thick. Cool a few minutes. Place chilled canned ham on rack over shallow pan; spoon glaze over. Chill till glaze is set. Slice and serve.

Ham-Platter Meal

    1 24-ounce canned ham
    1 18-ounce can whole sweet potatoes
    4 spiced peach halves
    1 10-ounce package frozen peas, cooked

Slice ham in fourths; place in center of broiler pan. Arrange sweet potatoes and peach halves around ham. Spread over all a mixture of ½ cup each brown sugar and liquid from spiced peaches.

Broil about 7 minutes. Turn; brush with 2 tablespoons melted butter and broil 7 more minutes. Arrange on platter with the drained peas. Makes 4 servings.

Fruited Luncheon Loaf

Slice one 12-ounce can luncheon meat in ¼-inch slices to within 1 inch of bottom. Place in shallow baking pan. Peel and section two large oranges; poke sections between slices of meat, fan-fashion. Pour over your favorite raisin sauce. Bake at 375° about 20 minutes, basting occasionally. Serves 4.

Green-pepper Boats

    4 large green peppers
    ½ cup chopped onion
    2 tablespoons butter or margarine
    2 cups cooked rice
    1 can condensed cream of celery soup
    ½ teaspoon salt
    Dash pepper
    Few drops Tabasco sauce
    1 4½-ounce can deviled ham

Remove tops and seeds from peppers; precook 5 minutes. Drain. Cook onion in butter till tender but not brown. Combine onion, rice, soup, and seasonings; fill peppers with rice mixture. Make a well in rice; fill with deviled ham. Place peppers upright in shallow baking dish; add small amount water to cover bottom of dish. Bake at 350° about 30 minutes. Makes 4 servings.

Deviled-ham Bean Bake

    ½ cup sliced onion, separated in rings
    1 tablespoon fat
    1 4½-ounce can deviled ham
    1 tablespoon molasses
    1 teaspoon prepared mustard
    Dash salt
    1 1-pound can (2 cups) Boston style
        pork and beans
    1 medium tomato, peeled and sliced or
    1 cup well-drained canned tomatoes

Cook onion in hot fat till tender but not brown. Combine deviled ham, molasses, mustard, salt, and beans.

In 1-quart casserole, alternate layers of bean mixture with onion and tomato. Bake in moderate oven (350°) about 30 minutes. Makes 6 to 8 servings.

↑

Glazed Canned Ham is sliced before baking—easy to serve

Easy because the last-minute fuss of carving is already done—ham travels straight from oven to buffet. Meat is delicious, too—glaze bastes each slice.

← When you set off to buy this easy-to-serve ham, take along a shallow baking pan, or heavy foil. Ask meatman to slice canned ham, tie with heavy cord, and place in pan. (Or slice canned ham on your own food-slicing machine.)

Bake ham in a slow oven (325°) for about 20 minutes *per pound* for small canned ham (about 6 pounds); 15 minutes *per pound* for larger ham (8 to 13 pounds). Last 30 minutes, cover with orange marmalade; continue baking till glazed. Place on platter; remove cord.

Saucy Corned-beef Patties

2 tablespoons chopped onion
1½ teaspoons butter or margarine
½ cup seasoned tomato sauce
2 tablespoons chopped green pepper
1 tablespoon Worcestershire sauce
1½ teaspoons sugar
1 1-pound can (2 cups) corned-beef
    hash, chilled

Cook onion in butter till tender; add all ingredients except hash; heat thoroughly.

Slice hash in fourths. Broil 2 inches from heat 8 to 10 minutes, or till brown and crusty. Serve with sauce. Makes 4 servings.

Corned-beef Pie

1 1-pound can (2 cups) corned-beef hash
½ cup catsup
1 slightly beaten egg
1 10-ounce package frozen Limas, cooked
¼ pound sharp process American
    cheese, shredded (1 cup)
2 tablespoons milk

Combine hash, catsup, and egg; press into bottom and sides of greased 8-inch pieplate. Bake at 350° about 30 minutes. Fill crust with Limas. Heat cheese and milk over *very low heat*, stirring constantly, till cheese melts. Pour over Limas; cut in 6 wedges.

Pizza Hash

1 1-pound can corned-beef hash, chilled
¼ pound sharp process American
    cheese, shredded (1 cup)
1 8-ounce can (1 cup) seasoned tomato
    sauce
1 3-ounce can (⅔ cup) broiled chopped
    mushrooms, drained
½ teaspoon garlic salt
½ teaspon crushed oregano
2 tablespoons grated Parmesan cheese

Cut hash in 6 slices; arrange in 11x7x1½-inch baking dish. Sprinkle American cheese over hash. Combine tomato sauce, mushrooms, garlic salt, and oregano; spoon over hash. Sprinkle with Parmesan cheese. Bake in moderate oven (375°) about 20 minutes or till hot through. Makes 3 servings.

Squaw Corn

Cube one 12-ounce can luncheon meat; brown the cubes in a little hot fat.

Combine 3 slightly beaten eggs, one 1-pound can (2 cups) golden cream-style corn, ¼ teaspoon salt, and dash of pepper; add to meat. Cook over low heat, stirring occasionally, just till the eggs are set. Serve immediately, sprinkled with chopped chives. Makes 6 servings.

Pizza Hash is an Italian version of corned-beef hash. You can fix it in 30 minutes—hash comes from a can. Add a zesty cheese topper and bake in a tomato sauce seasoned with oregano.

*Luncheon meat's
a 20-minute meal
for busy day*

20-minute Banquet: Slice each of three 12-ounce cans luncheon meat in fourths, *cutting only ¾ way through.* Place in shallow pan; spread with orange marmalade. Add canned potatoes brushed with butter. Bake at 375° 20 minutes. Sprinkle spuds with chopped parsley.

Dried-beef Dinner

¼ pound (2 cups) dried beef*, shredded
2 tablespoons butter or margarine

. . .

2 tablespoons enriched flour
1 cup milk
½ teaspoon Worcestershire sauce
Dash pepper
Chow-mein noodles, baked potatoes,
    or hot toast points

Cook dried beef in butter till edges frizzle. Push meat to one side; blend flour and butter. Slowly add milk; cook, stirring constantly till thick, gradually including the dried beef. Add Worcestershire sauce and pepper. Season with salt if needed.

Spoon over crisp chow-mein noodles from a can, baked potatoes, or hot toast points. Makes 4 servings.

*If dried beef is extra salty, let stand a few minutes in boiling water. Drain on paper towels before cooking in the butter.

Macaroni in Meat Sauce

⅔ cup chopped celery
½ cup chopped onion
1 clove garlic, minced
2 tablespoons fat
1 12-ounce can luncheon meat,
    cut in sticks
1 can condensed tomato soup
1 soup can water
1 teaspoon salt
¼ teaspoon pepper

. . .

½ 6-ounce package (1 cup)
    7-minute macaroni

Cook celery, onion, and garlic in hot fat till tender but not brown. Add luncheon meat and brown lightly.

Add remaining ingredients except macaroni. Simmer, uncovered, 20 minutes. Add macaroni; cover and continue cooking 15 minutes or till macaroni is done. Serve with grated Parmesan cheese.

Makes 4 to 6 servings.

Easy Chicken a la King

¼ cup chopped green pepper
2 tablespoons diced celery
2 tablespoons butter or margarine
1 tablespoon enriched flour
1 can condensed cream of chicken soup
2 3-ounce cans (1⅛ cups) broiled,
   sliced mushrooms
1 5½-ounce can (¾ cup) chicken, diced
¼ cup chopped pimiento
¼ teaspoon monosodium glutamate
Salt and pepper

Cook green pepper and celery in butter till tender. Blend in flour; gradually add soup; add mushrooms and liquid. Cook, stirring constantly, till thick. Add chicken, pimiento, and seasonings; heat thoroughly. Serve over hot toast. Makes 4 to 6 servings.

Jiffy Mexican Dinner

¼ cup chopped onion
¼ cup chopped green pepper
1 11-ounce can tamales
1 1-pound can (2 cups) chili con carne
   with beans
½ cup shredded sharp American cheese

Cook onion and green pepper in hot fat till tender. Add chili. Remove shucks from tamales; arrange spoke-fashion on top. Cover; heat 10 to 15 minutes. Sprinkle with cheese and serve. Makes 4 or 5 servings.

Bologna Bake

¾ pound Bologna, diced (2 cups)
1 cup celery slices
¼ cup sliced stuffed green olives
4 hard-cooked eggs, diced
¼ cup chopped onion
1 tablespoon prepared mustard
Dash pepper
¾ cup mayonnaise
1 cup crushed potato chips

Combine all ingredients except potato chips. Place in 8x1¾-inch round baking dish; sprinkle with crushed potato chips. Bake in hot oven (400°) 20 to 25 minutes or until hot. Makes 4 or 5 servings.

Bologna Baskets

Heat double-thick slices of Bologna in a little hot fat just till meat "cups." Fill hot cups with potato salad.

Rotisserie Bologna

Buy unsliced big Bologna (the amount depends on crowd and size of rotisserie). Remove skin if you like and score surface. Center Bologna lengthwise on spit; adjust in rotisserie.

Broil meat till heated and nicely browned —about 1½ hours for 5 or 6 pounds.

Sausage 'n Peach Special

Drain 1 No. 2½ can (3½ cups) peach halves. Sprinkle each peach half with brown sugar. Broil 3 inches from heat 5 minutes. Put chili sauce in each peach half; top with 2 Vienna sausages. Broil 8 to 10 minutes more. Makes 6 to 8 servings.

Pigs in Blankets

Pat out refrigerated biscuits lengthwise. Roll each around a canned Vienna sausage; fasten with toothpick or seal edges with fingers. Bake at 425° about 12 to 15 minutes. Spoon creamed peas over and serve as main dish. Without peas, they're hot appetizers.

Quick meals with canned meat cut-up

Tiny Fruit-glazed Loaves. Cut loaf of canned luncheon meat in half and you have two little meat loaves! Place loaves, rounded side up, in shallow baking pan.

Spread each tiny loaf with 2 tablespoons cranberry sauce, applesauce, orange marmalade, or peach preserves. Bake in moderate oven (350°) about 20 minutes or till heated through.

Canned sweet potatoes may be baked alongside — brush with melted butter and sprinkle with a little brown sugar.

Busy-day Barbecue stars strips of canned luncheon meat. Chef's tip: Cut loaf lengthwise in ¼-inch slices. Stack three or four slices and cut in thin strips.

Cook ¾ cup onion slices in a little hot fat till tender. Add 1 cup catsup, ¼ cup sugar, ¼ cup Worcestershire sauce, 1 tablespoon vinegar, ½ teaspoon salt.

Add one 12-ounce can luncheon meat cut in thin strips; heat to boiling. Spoon the meat sauce over hot fluffy rice. Makes 3 or 4 servings.

Speedy Kabobs—canned luncheon meat with a party flair! String skewers with chunks of the meat and pineapple, green-pepper squares, and tomato wedges while the zippy sauce is bubbling.

Speedy Kabobs

    4 10-inch skewers
    1 12-ounce can luncheon meat, cut in
        12 cubes
    1 green pepper, cut in 12 squares
    12 canned or frozen pineapple chunks
    1 recipe Kabob Sauce
    2 medium tomatoes, quartered

On skewers alternate meat, green pepper, and pineapple. Brush generously with Kabob Sauce. Broil 5 to 6 inches from heat 8 to 9 minutes, or till lightly browned. Turn; place tomatoes on ends of skewers. Brush all with sauce; broil 4 to 5 minutes more. Serve immediately with remaining sauce. Makes 4 servings.

Kabob Sauce: Combine one 8-ounce can (1 cup) seasoned tomato sauce, ½ cup pineapple syrup (drained from chunks), ¼ cup finely chopped green onions, ¼ cup butter, 1 teaspoon Worcestershire sauce, 1 teaspoon monosodium glutamate, and ½ teaspoon salt. Simmer 15 minutes or till thick.

Beef 'n Potato Bake

    1 1-pound can brown gravy and
        sliced beef*
    ¼ cup chopped onion
    Packaged instant mashed potato
    ½ cup shredded process American
        cheese

Spread meat and gravy in 8x1¾-inch round baking dish. Sprinkle onion over. Bake at 425° about 10 minutes or till hot.

Meanwhile, prepare the instant potato (enough for 4 servings) according to package directions, but add last of liquid slowly so you can omit a little if necessary to make potatoes stiff enough to hold their shape. Drop hot potatoes by spoonfuls over meat, making 4 mounds; sprinkle with cheese.

Return to oven and bake 3 minutes longer or till cheese melts. Makes 4 servings.

(For double recipe, use an 8x8x2-inch baking dish. Heat 18 minutes before adding potatoes and cheese; bake 3 minutes more.)

*Or use one 12-ounce can roast beef, and thicken meat broth for gravy.

All kinds and cuts of poultry

Roast Stuffed Turkey

Stuff and truss turkey just before roasting—¾ to 1 cup Parsley Stuffing (page 90) per pound ready-to-cook weight. Stuff wishbone cavity and skewer neck skin to back. Tuck wing tips behind shoulder joints. Rub large cavity with salt. Spoon in stuffing. Shake bird to settle stuffing; do not pack.

Place skewers across opening; lace shut with cord. Tie drumsticks securely to tail. (If opening has band of skin across, push the drumsticks underneath, and you won't need to fasten openings or tie legs.)

Grease skin thoroughly. If you use a meat thermometer, insert it in the center of the inside thigh muscle adjoining the cavity.

To roast: Place bird breast up on rack or in V-rack in shallow roasting pan; leave in this position for entire roasting time. Cover with loose "cap" of foil—press lightly at drumstick and breast ends, but *avoid having it touch top or sides.* Roast according to chart below.

Turkey roasting timetable

Set oven at 325°. Times are for chilled turkeys stuffed just before roasting—

Ready-to-cook weight (before stuffing)	Time* (total)
6 to 8 lbs.	3½ to 4 hrs.
8 to 12 lbs.	4 to 4½ hrs.
12 to 16 lbs.	4½ to 5½ hrs.
16 to 20 lbs.	5½ to 6½ hrs.
20 to 24 lbs.	6½ to 7½ hrs.

Foil-wrapped-turkey roasting timetable

Set oven at 450°. Times are for unstuffed chilled turkeys. For stuffed turkey, add 30 to 45 minutes to total roasting time.

Ready-to-cook weight (before stuffing)	Time* (total)
8 to 10 lbs.	2¼ to 2½ hrs.
10 to 13 lbs.	2½ to 3 hrs.
13 to 17 lbs.	3 to 3¼ hrs.
17 to 21 lbs.	3¼ to 3½ hrs.
21 to 24 lbs.	3½ to 3¾ hrs.

*Cooking times are approximate only. Meat thermometer should register 195° (for Foil-wrapped Roast Turkey, 190°).

When turkey is about two-thirds done according to timetable, cut cord or band of skin so heat can reach inside of thighs.

Doneness tests: About 20 minutes before roasting time is up, test doneness by pressing thick part of drumstick between fingers (protect with paper towel). Meat should feel soft. Move drumstick up and down; it should move easily or twist out of joint. (Thermometer should register 195°.)

When turkey is done, remove from pan and keep warm while you make gravy from pan drippings. Let turkey stand 20 minutes. Carving is easier, slices neater.

Foil-wrapped Roast Turkey

Truss and wrap: Tie drumsticks to tail. Press wings to body so tips are flat against sides of breast. Place turkey, breast up, in center of heavy foil. (Foil should be wide enough to have 5 to 6 inches extending beyond each end of bird; if it isn't, join 2 pieces together with drugstore or lock fold, pressing to make leakproof joining.)

Bring one end of foil snugly over top of turkey; bring opposite end up, lapping over first (overlap should be 2 to 3 inches). Fold foil down snugly at breast and legs; then press remaining two sides of foil up—high enough to prevent drippings from running into pan and burning.

To roast: Place foil-wrapped bird, breast up, in bottom of shallow pan (broiler pan is convenient)—don't use rack. Roast at constant high temperature—see the Foil-wrapped-turkey roasting timetable at left.

When turkey has cooked to within *15 to 20 minutes of total cooking time* given in timetable, *remove from oven.* Quickly slit foil with scissors or knife and fold away from bird to edge of pan. (If you use meat thermometer, insert now in center of inside thigh muscle adjoining cavity.)

Return turkey to oven and roast till tender—see doneness tests above (thermometer should read 195°). When turkey's done, lift from foil to warm platter. Pour drippings in skillet; to increase flavor and color, concentrate by simmering; make gravy.

Roast Stuffed Turkey

Admire him first, golden brown and crusty, magnificent on the platter. Dad carves tender slices, spoons out fragrant stuffing. Mother serves mashed potatoes. Giblet Gravy makes its round.

Turkey carving helps—sharp knife, sturdy fork, big platter

1 Place turkey, legs to your right. First carve far side. Hold drumstick with fingers. Cut the joint joining the leg to the backbone.

2 Hold leg on plate. Cut joint to separate drumstick, thigh. Slice drumstick, turning for even slices. Slice the thigh parallel to bone.

3 To cut white meat, first make deep cut into breast to body frame, parallel to and close to wing. Anchor turkey with fork.

4 Starting halfway up breast, thinly slice white meat down to cut made above wing. Take stuffing from opening where leg was removed.

Parsley Stuffing

3 quarts slightly dry bread cubes
1 teaspoon ground sage
1 teaspoon thyme
1 teaspoon rosemary
1½ teaspoons salt
⅓ cup chopped parsley
⅓ cup finely chopped onion
⅓ cup butter or margarine, melted
1 cup canned chicken broth

Combine all ingredients except broth. Add broth; toss lightly to mix. Makes 8 cups, or enough to stuff a 12-pound turkey.

Frozen Turkey (*unstuffed*)

Thaw frozen unstuffed turkey in original wrapping shortly before time to cook. To speed up thawing, you can place wrapped turkey under cold running water. See label directions that come with turkey.

Thawing timetable for frozen turkeys (unstuffed)

Ready-to-cook weight	In refrigerator (40°)
4 to 12 lbs.	1 to 2 days
12 to 20 lbs.	2 to 3 days
20 to 24 lbs.	3 to 4 days

Roast Quarter of Turkey
(*Foil-roasted*)

A quarter-turkey roast may vary from 4½ to 7 pounds, ready-to-cook weight. (Allow about ½ pound per serving.) For all white meat, choose a forequarter. A drumstick quarter gives mostly dark meat. *Frozen roast:* Before cooking, thaw completely in refrigerator (takes about 1½ to 3 days).

To truss: *Forequarter*—tie cord around breast end to hold the wing flat. *Drumstick quarter*—tuck the white-meat piece under leg and tie leg to tail or body.

Foil-wrap: Rub cut side of turkey with salt. Place trussed roast, skin side up, on square of heavy foil. Bring one end of foil snugly over top of turkey; bring opposite end up lapping over first (overlap should be 2 to 3 inches). Then press remaining two sides of foil up—high enough to prevent drippings from running into pan.

To roast: Place foil-wrapped roast in shallow pan—don't use rack. Roast in very hot oven (450°) 20 to 25 minutes *per pound*.

When turkey has cooked to within *15 to 20 minutes of total cooking time, remove from oven.* Quickly slit foil, fold away from roast. (If you use a meat thermometer, insert it in center of thickest meaty section of forequarter; or in center of inside thigh muscle.) Roast till tender. Test for doneness—see page 88. (Thermometer should register 190°.)

A casserole of stuffing (covered) may be placed in oven last half hour of roasting.

Frozen Stuffed Turkey—oven-ready in less than 10 minutes

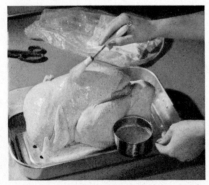

Buy stuffed and frozen bird. Keep frozen till ready to cook. Remove plastic bag; follow enclosed cooking directions. Place bird breast up on rack in shallow pan. Brush with melted fat.

Cover loosely with cap of foil—tuck in at both ends of bird. This prevents too rapid browning of breast, keeps turkey moist. Don't add water; you may leave roasting pan uncovered.

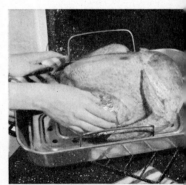

Test bird for doneness — page 88. To cut roasting time about 1 hour, transfer turkey from freezer to refrigerator night before.

Turkey-stuffing time? Just follow these picture steps

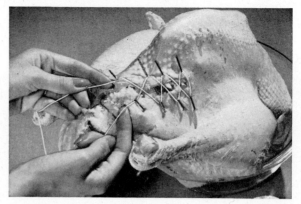

Fill wishbone cavity with stuffing; skewer neck skin to back. Rub large cavity with salt; spoon in stuffing — *do not pack;* shake down to settle.

To close cavity, hold edges of skin together with lacing pins or skewers. With heavy cord, lace cavity shut. Bake extra stuffing (covered) the last half hour of roasting; baste occasionally with pan drippings.

Fried Turkey Cutups

½ cup enriched flour
2 teaspoons salt
2 teaspoons paprika
¼ teaspoon pepper
1 fryer-roaster turkey, 3½ to 6 pounds, ready-to-cook weight, cut in pieces

Combine flour and seasonings. Rub into turkey pieces. Dry on rack. Slowly brown a few pieces at a time in ½ inch hot fat in large skillet—takes 15 to 20 minutes for each batch. Return all browned pieces to skillet, reduce heat and cover tightly.* Cook about 1 hour or till tender. Uncover last 10 minutes to crisp. Makes 6 to 8 servings.

*If cover is not tight, add 1 to 2 tablespoons water.

Oven-fried Turkey

1 fryer-roaster turkey, 3½ to 6 pounds, ready-to-cook weight, cut in pieces
1¼ cups butter or margarine, melted
2 cups crushed packaged herb-stuffing

Sprinkle turkey pieces with salt and pepper. Dip in butter; roll in crushed herb-stuffing. Place pieces skin side up in jelly-roll pan. Drizzle half of remaining butter over turkey; sprinkle with rest of crumbs.

Bake at 350° 1 hour and 40 minutes or till tender. After about 1 hour of baking drizzle with remaining butter. Serves 4 to 7.

Fricassee of Turkey

½ cup packaged pancake mix
¼ cup corn meal
1½ tablespoons salt
½ teaspoon pepper
5 to 6 pounds large turkey wings and drumsticks (4 pieces in all)*
1 can condensed consomme

Combine pancake mix, corn meal, salt, and pepper. Cut wings apart at joints making flat pieces. Coat turkey pieces with flour mixture. Brown slowly in ¼ inch hot fat in Dutch oven. Pour off excess fat. Add consomme. Cover; bake at 325° about 2 hours.

Ladle some of pan gravy over Mushroom Wild Rice. Makes 4 or 5 generous servings.

*If frozen, thaw completely in refrigerator (takes about 1 day) before cooking.

Mushroom Wild Rice

Prepare ½ cup wild rice according to package directions (allow over an hour). Drain 1 6-ounce can broiled sliced mushrooms, reserving liquid; add enough water to mushroom liquid to make 1⅓ cups. Add ½ teaspoon salt; use as liquid for preparing 1⅓ cups packaged precooked rice; heat according to package directions.

Combine drained wild rice, hot precooked rice, mushrooms, and 2 tablespoons butter or margarine. Cover; heat over *low* heat.

Rock Cornish Game Hens

To roast:

4 1-pound ready-to-cook Rock
   Cornish game hens
Salt and pepper
⅓ cup melted butter or margarine
· · ·
¼ cup canned condensed consomme
¼ cup light corn syrup

Season hens inside and out with salt and pepper. Stuff each with ¼ cup stuffing, if desired. Place, breast side up, on rack in shallow roasting pan and brush well with butter. Roast uncovered in hot oven (400°) about 1 hour, or till tender.

During last 15 minutes of baking time, baste several times with mixture of consomme and syrup. Makes 4 servings.

To broil: Split birds in half lengthwise. Place skin side down in broiler pan (not rack); brush with melted butter. Season with salt and pepper.

Broil 7 to 9 inches from heat about 30 minutes or till tender and drumstick moves up and down easily. Turn once; baste frequently. One bird makes 2 servings.

Squab

To roast: Clean 4 squabs. Rub inside with salt, pepper. Brown giblets; add to ½ recipe Fluffy Bread Stuffing (page 94); stuff squab; rub skin with butter. Place breast up on rack in shallow pan; roast uncovered in moderate oven (350°) till tender, 45 to 60 minutes. Makes 4 servings.

To broil: Follow directions for Broiled Rock Cornish Game Hens. Broil 5 to 7 inches from heat for total of 20 to 30 minutes. Serve on buttered toast.

Roast Goose

Clean goose and stuff with Fluffy Bread Stuffing, page 95. Place breast up on rack in shallow roasting pan. Pour 2 cups boiling water over and cover. Roast at 325° about 25 to 30 minutes *per pound*. Prick legs and wings with fork so fat will run out. Roast uncovered last 15 minutes.

To remove excess fat, goose may be precooked before roasting.

Roast Duckling

3½- to 5-pound ready-to-cook duckling
  or 5- to 7-pound dressed duckling
Salt
Orange Stuffing
· · ·
2 tablespoons honey
1 teaspoon kitchen bouquet
Kumquat flowers

Clean duckling: remove wing joints and tips, leaving only meaty second joints. Rub inside with salt. Stuff lightly with Orange Stuffing. Do not truss or prick skin. Close opening with skewers; lace shut with cord.

Place duckling breast up on rack in shallow roasting pan. Do not add water. Roast uncovered in slow oven (325°) 1½ to 2 hours for moderately done, 2 to 2½ hours for well done. Meaty part of leg should feel tender (protect hand with paper towel) and leg should move up and down easily.

Combine honey and kitchen bouquet for glaze; brush on duckling about 30 minutes before end of roasting time.

Remove to heated platter and trim with Kumquat Flowers. Makes 3 or 4 servings.

Orange Stuffing

3 cups toasted bread cubes
2 cups finely diced celery
1 tablespoon grated orange peel
⅔ cup diced orange sections
¾ teaspoon salt
½ teaspoon poultry seasoning
Dash pepper
1 beaten egg
¼ cup melted butter or margarine

Toss together bread, celery, orange peel, diced orange sections, and seasonings. Combine egg and butter; add to bread mixture, tossing lightly. Makes enough stuffing for a 5-pound duckling.

Kumquat Flowers

Leave kumquat whole. Make 4 petals by cutting peel in fourths from blossom end, going *almost* to stem end. Peel petals about ¾ way back. (Leave fruit portion as it is—it makes the center of the flower.)

Place in ice water about 1 hour or till petals have opened as much as you like. (The longer kumquats are in ice water, the further back the petals will curl.)

Variations of Perfect Gravy

Saucepan Method: Pour off fat from roasting pan. Combine fat and flour in saucepan. Add the liquid to roasting pan; simmer and stir till meat drippings dissolve. Add to saucepan. Cook and stir as below.

Brown Gravy: Stir flour into drippings; brown over low heat. Add kitchen bouquet.

Giblet Gravy: Add chopped cooked giblets; use giblet broth for part of liquid.

Hurry-up Gravy with Soup

Remove meat from roasting pan. Pour drippings in measuring cup; skim off fat. Pour 1 can condensed cream of chicken or cream of mushroom soup into pan. Stir well to loosen crusty bits on bottom of pan.

Blend in ¼ cup water and 3 tablespoons drippings. Cook over low heat, stirring constantly. Thin with more water, if necessary. Makes about 1½ cups gravy.

Perfect Gravy, step by step—rich, brown, and delicious

1 Lift roast to heated platter, keep warm. Leaving crusty bits in pan, pour off fat, meat juices. When fat comes to top, skim off. For each cup of gravy, measure 2 tablespoons fat back into pan.

2 For 2 cups gravy—6 to 8 servings—measure ¼ cup fat into pan, then stir in same amount of flour (2 tablespoons per cup gravy). Blend fat and flour. Cook and stir on *very low* heat till frothy.

3 Important tip: Remove pan from heat. Pour in liquid all at once—1 cup per cup of gravy, here it's 2 cups. Blend. (Use meat juices plus water, milk, or cream; or broth from poultry giblets.)

4 Stir in crusty bits. Return pan to heat. Season with salt, pepper, and monosodium glutamate—perhaps a dash of rosemary. Add a bit of kitchen bouquet. Simmer about 5 minutes and serve.

Chicken favorites – plain and fancy

Rolled Chicken Washington

½ cup finely chopped fresh mushrooms
   or 1 3-ounce can (⅔ cup) broiled
   chopped mushrooms, drained
2 tablespoons butter or margarine
2 tablespoons all-purpose flour
½ cup light cream
¼ teaspoon salt
Dash cayenne pepper
1¼ cups shredded sharp Cheddar cheese
6 or 7 boned whole chicken breasts
All-purpose flour
2 slightly beaten eggs
¾ cup fine dry bread crumbs

For cheese filling: Cook mushrooms in butter, about 5 minutes. Blend in flour; stir in cream. Add salt and cayenne; cook and stir until mixture becomes very thick. Stir in cheese; cook over very low heat, stirring constantly, until cheese is melted. Turn mixture into pie plate. Cover; chill thoroughly, about 1 hour. Cut the firm cheese mixture into 6 or 7 equal portions; shape it into short sticks. If not already done, remove skin from chicken breasts. To make cutlets, place each piece of chicken, boned side up, between two pieces of saran. (Overlap meat where chicken breast is split.) Working out from the center, pound with wood mallet to form cutlets not quite ¼ inch thick. (Or ask your meatman to flatten the chicken breasts for you.) Peel off saran. Sprinkle meat with salt. Place a cheese stick on each chicken breast. Tucking in the sides, roll chicken as for jellyroll. Press to seal well.

Dust the chicken rolls with flour; dip in slightly beaten egg, then roll in fine dry bread crumbs. Cover and chill chicken rolls thoroughly—at least 1 hour. (Or fix ahead and chill overnight.) About an hour before serving time, fry rolls in deep, hot fat (375°) for 5 minutes or till crisp and golden brown; drain on absorbent paper towels. Place rolls in shallow baking dish and bake in slow oven (325°) about 30 to 45 minutes. Serve on warm platter. Makes 6 or 7 servings.

Tender crisp elegance

Serve Rolled Chicken Washington as prepared on one of the country's major air lines. It's a masterpiece of tender chicken rolled around a delicious cheese filling.

Sesame-baked Chicken

Add a touch of the exotic to your next oven-fried chicken. It's beautifully crisp outside, moist and tender inside—

⅔ cup fine cracker crumbs
   (15 crackers)
¼ cup toasted sesame seed*
   • • •
1 2½- to 3-pound ready-to-cook
   broiler-fryer, cut up
½ 6-ounce can (⅓ cup) evaporated
   milk
½ cup butter or margarine, melted
Parsley

Combine cracker crumbs and toasted sesame seed. Dip chicken pieces in evaporated milk, then roll in cracker mixture. Pour melted butter into 11½x7½x1½-inch baking dish. Dip skin side of chicken pieces in butter; turn over and arrange, skin side up, in baking dish. Bake uncovered in a moderate oven (350°) for 1½ hours or till done. Remove to warm serving platter; garnish with parsley. Makes 3 or 4 servings.

*To toast sesame seed, place in a shallow, ungreased baking pan. Heat in a moderate oven (350°) for about 10 minutes, stirring once or twice to toast evenly.

Skillet Cherry Chicken

1 12-ounce jar (1 cup) cherry
   preserves
2 tablespoons lemon juice
4 whole cloves
¼ teaspoon salt
¼ teaspoon allspice
¼ teaspoon mace
   • • •
½ cup all-purpose flour
1 teaspoon salt
1 2½- to 3-pound ready-to-cook
   broiler-fryer, cut up
¼ cup salad oil

Blend together cherry preserves, lemon juice, cloves, salt, allspice, and mace; set aside. Combine flour and salt in paper or plastic bag. Add 2 or 3 pieces of chicken at a time; shake to coat. Brown chicken in oil in skillet over medium heat, turning with tongs. Cover; cook 15 minutes. Drain off fat; add cherry sauce. Cover; simmer, over very low heat, skin side up 15 minutes. Turn; simmer 15 minutes longer or till tender. Makes 4 servings.

Chicken—it's always special

Party Chicken

4 chicken breasts
¼ cup enriched flour
½ teaspoon salt
¼ teaspoon paprika

• • •

2 cups dry bread cubes
1 tablespoon chopped onion
½ teaspoon salt
¼ teaspoon poultry seasoning
Dash pepper
2 tablespoons butter, melted
¼ cup hot water
½ cup butter or margarine, melted
1 recipe Mushroom Sauce

Split chicken breasts just enough to fold. Combine flour, ½ teaspoon salt, paprika, and dash pepper in paper bag; add chicken and shake to coat.

For stuffing: Combine bread cubes, onion, ½ teaspoon salt, poultry seasoning, and pepper. Add 2 tablespoons butter and hot water; toss gently to moisten.

Fill cavity of each piece of chicken with stuffing. Hold stuffing in by skewering opening shut with toothpicks. Dip chicken in the ½ cup melted butter; place in baking dish. (Drizzle any remaining butter over top.)

Bake in slow oven (325°) 45 minutes; turn, and bake an additional 45 minutes, or till tender. Sprinkle with chopped parsley. Serve with Mushroom Sauce. Serves 4.

Mushroom Sauce

½ pound fresh mushrooms,
   cut in half
¼ cup minced onion
2 tablespoons butter or margarine
1 to 2 tablespoons enriched flour
½ cup heavy cream
½ cup dairy sour cream
½ teaspoon salt
¼ teaspoon pepper

Cook mushrooms and onion lightly in butter till tender but not brown; cover and cook 10 minutes over low heat. Push mushrooms to one side and stir flour into butter. Add heavy cream, sour cream, and seasonings. Heat slowly, stirring constantly, almost to boiling point. Makes about 1½ cups.

Orange-glazed Chicken 'n Rice

1 2½- or 3-pound ready-to-cook young
   chicken, cut in pieces
½ 6-ounce can frozen orange-juice
   concentrate
2 tablespoons butter or margarine
½ teaspoon ginger
1 cup water
1 tablespoon orange-juice concentrate
1 cup packaged precooked rice
2 tablespoons seedless raisins
½ teaspoon salt
2 tablespoons toasted slivered
   blanched almonds

Sprinkle chicken with salt and pepper. Place pieces, skin side up and not touching, in foil-lined jelly-roll pan. Bake in moderate oven (350°) 30 minutes—need not turn.

In saucepan, combine ½ cup concentrate, butter, ginger; heat; spoon over chicken. Bake 30 minutes longer or till tender.

Meanwhile, make *Raisin Rice:* Mix water and the 1 tablespoon orange-juice concentrate; bring to boiling. Add rice, raisins, and salt; then proceed according to directions on rice package. Sprinkle with almonds. Serve with chicken. Makes 4 servings.

Yorkshire Chicken

⅓ cup enriched flour
2 teaspoons salt
1½ teaspoons ground sage
¼ teaspoon pepper
1 2½- to 3-pound ready-to-cook young
   chicken, cut in pieces
¼ cup fat
1 cup sifted enriched flour
1 teaspoon baking powder
1 teaspoon salt
3 well-beaten eggs
1½ cups milk
¼ cup butter or margarine, melted
¼ cup chopped parsley

Combine first 4 ingredients; coat chicken. Brown in hot fat; place in 2-quart casserole.

Sift 1 cup flour, the baking powder, and 1 teaspoon salt. Combine eggs, milk, butter, parsley; add to flour mixture; stir till smooth. Pour over chicken. Bake at 350° about 1 hour. Makes 4 or 5 servings.

Chicken Cacciatore

  1 3-pound ready-to-cook young chicken
  2 medium onions, cut in ¼-inch slices
  1 1-pound can (2 cups) tomatoes
  1 8-ounce can seasoned tomato sauce
  1 to 2 cloves garlic, minced
  1 teaspoon salt
  ¼ teaspoon pepper
  ½ teaspoon celery seed
  1 teaspoon crushed oregano
  1 or 2 bay leaves

Cut up chicken, brown in ¼ cup hot olive oil; remove from skillet. Add onion; cook over low heat till golden. Drain off fat.

Add remaining ingredients. Add chicken; cover, and simmer 45 minutes. Uncover and cook, turning chicken occasionally, till chicken is tender and sauce is thick, about 20 minutes. Skim off excess fat and remove bay leaves. Makes 4 to 6 servings.

Orange-spiced Peaches

Drain one No. 2½ can peach halves, reserving ½ cup syrup. In cheesecloth, tie 1 teaspoon whole cloves, 6 inches stick cinnamon, and 10 whole allspice. Combine syrup, ⅓ cup vinegar, ½ cup sugar, ½ large orange sliced, peaches, and spices. Heat to boiling; simmer uncovered 5 minutes. Cover; let cool to room temperature. Remove spice bag. Stud with whole cloves.

Golden Broiled Chicken

Select 2 ready-to-cook young chickens (not over 2½ pounds each). Split in half lengthwise. Break wing, hip, and drumstick joints so birds will stay flat during broiling.

Brush with melted fat or salad oil. Season with 2 teaspoons salt and ½ teaspoon each pepper and monosodium glutamate.

Broil skin side down, 5 to 7 inches from heat, about 25 minutes or till lightly browned. Brush occasionally with fat. Turn; broil 15 to 20 minutes longer. When drumstick cuts easily and no pink shows, chicken is done. Makes 4 servings.

Island Broiled Chicken

  1 cup salad oil
  ⅓ cup lemon juice
  3 tablespoons soy sauce
  1 clove garlic, minced
  1 teaspoon oregano
  1 teaspoon monosodium glutamate
  ½ teaspoon salt
  ¼ teaspoon pepper
        • • •
  2 ready-to-cook young chickens (about
      2 pounds each), split in half

Combine all ingredients except chicken; let chicken chill in sauce 4 or 5 hours. Broil as for Golden Broiled Chicken, brushing occasionally with sauce. Makes 4 servings.

Party Chicken—company delicious

Lavishly buttered chicken breasts, plumped with moist herbed stuffing, rate extra good top-off— rich creamy Mushroom Sauce! Orange-spiced Peaches (recipe above) are the fragrant relish. Serve them hot or cold—good with ham, too.

How to stew a chicken

Choose a 4- to 5-pound ready-to-cook chicken or 2 "bro-hens" (older broiler-fryers), 2½ to 3 pounds each. In Dutch oven, place back, wings, legs; white meat atop. Or cook whole.

Add water just to cover. (If chicken is for salad, use ½ cup water per pound.) Add salt — ½ teaspoon *per pound* of chicken.

Add stalk of celery, 1 onion, 1 carrot, 4 whole black peppers, 2 whole cloves, 2 whole all-spice, and 1 bay leaf. Bring to boiling, reduce heat; *simmer* 3 to 4 hours (2½ to 3 hours for "bro-hens") or till tender. Remove chicken from broth; cool both immediately and chill. Skim fat from the broth.

Gold Coast Chicken

1 lemon
¼ cup butter or margarine
¼ cup enriched flour
2½ cups chicken broth

• • •

2 beaten egg yolks
1 3-ounce can (⅔ cup) broiled sliced mushrooms
1 1-pound can large white asparagus tips, drained and cut in half
2 tablespoons drained capers

• • •

1 recipe Stewed Chicken, hot (see picture directions at left)

Pare lemon like an apple, going round and round so peel is in one long spiral. Then squeeze lemon, reserving 2 tablespoons juice. Melt butter and blend in flour. Slowly add broth. Cook and stir till thick.

Stir small amount of hot mixture into egg yolks, then return to hot mixture; add lemon-peel spiral. Cook and stir 1 minute. Add mushrooms (with liquid), reserved lemon juice, and asparagus. Heat thoroughly, stirring occasionally. Add capers.

Pour sauce over hot drained Stewed Chicken in serving dish. Trim with the jaunty twist of cooked lemon peel, fluffs of parsley.

Makes 6 servings.

Chicken a la King

¼ cup butter, margarine, or chicken fat, melted
3 tablespoons enriched flour
1 cup chicken broth
1 cup milk

• • •

½ teaspoon salt
2 cups diced cooked chicken
1 3-ounce can (⅔ cup) broiled sliced mushrooms, drained
¼ cup chopped pimiento

• • •

Hot toast points or popovers

Blend butter and flour. Slowly add broth and milk. Cook, stirring constantly, over low heat, till sauce is thick.

Add salt, chicken, mushrooms, and pimiento. Heat through. Serve over hot toast points or in popovers. Makes 5 servings.

Chicken-noodle Soup

Heat 3 cups broth from Stewed Chicken; add 1 cup noodles. Cook about 30 minutes or until noodles are tender. Makes 4 servings.

Sunday-best Chicken Orange

¾ cup enriched flour
2 teaspoons grated orange peel
1 teaspoon paprika
1 tablespoon salt
¼ teaspoon pepper
1 2½- or 3-pound ready-to-cook frying
  chicken, cut in pieces
Fat
2 tablespoons water
1 recipe Orange Sauce

Combine flour, orange peel, paprika, salt and pepper in paper or plastic bag; add 2 or 3 pieces chicken at a time and shake. (Reserve remaining flour mixture for gravy.) Place on rack to let coating dry. Heat fat (¼ inch deep in skillet) till it will sizzle a drop of water. Brown meaty pieces of chicken first; then slip others in. Brown one side slowly; turn. When lightly browned, 15 to 20 minutes, reduce heat; add water, cover; cook 30 to 35 minutes or till tender. Uncover last 10 minutes to crisp. Remove chicken to warm platter and serve with *Orange Sauce:* Pour off pan drippings, reserving 2 tablespoons. Blend in 3 tablespoons reserved flour mixture. Cook and stir till frothy. Remove from heat; stir in 1½ cups milk, ½ cup orange juice, ¼ teaspoon ginger, and dash allspice. Simmer sauce about 5 minutes. Season to taste with salt and pepper. Makes 4 servings.

Fricasseed Chicken

½ cup enriched flour
2 teaspoons salt
2 teaspoons paprika
1 2- to 3-pound ready-to-cook young
  chicken, cut in pieces, or 2 1-pound
  packages frozen chicken pieces
¼ cup fat
•   •   •
1 cup water
2 small onions, sliced
2 bay leaves
¼ cup chopped celery leaves
2 teaspoons salt
Dash pepper
•   •   •
Milk
⅓ cup enriched flour
½ teaspoon salt
¼ teaspoon kitchen bouquet

Mix flour, salt, and paprika; coat chicken. Brown in hot fat in skillet or pressure pan.

Add next 6 ingredients. In skillet, cook covered 1 hour or till tender; in pressure pan, cook at 15 pounds pressure 35 minutes; allow the pressure to go down normally.

Remove chicken. Strain broth; add milk to make 3 cups. Shake 1 cup of the liquid with ⅓ cup flour to blend. Add remaining liquid. Return to skillet or pressure pan. Cook and stir, till gravy is thick. Add ½ teaspoon salt and the kitchen bouquet. Pour over chicken. Makes 4 to 6 servings.

Sunday-best Chicken Orange

Fried Chicken fancied up with orange peel. Make the spicy gravy with orange juice and milk. Ladle over the golden chicken or pass in gravy boat.

Give mealtime a lift with fish and sea food

Boiled Lobster

Select active live lobsters. Plunge, head first, into boiling, salted water to cover. Bring back to boiling, cook 5 minutes; reduce heat, simmer 20 minutes. Remove at once. Crack shell; discard craw or crop near head, and black vein that runs to tail.

Serve lobster as main course—hot with butter, or split and chilled with mayonnaise. Or remove meat for hot creamed dishes, casseroles, chilled salads, or appetizers.

Broiled Lobster

Place lobster on back. Kill by cutting spinal cord between body and tail shells. With sharp knife split open from head to tail. Leave in green fat and red coral.

Discard craw or crop near head and remove black vein down tail section. Brush meat with melted butter or margarine; broil. (A 1¼-pound lobster takes 10 to 15 minutes.) Serve with melted butter. Allow ¾ to 1 pound lobster per person.

Boiled Frozen Rock-lobster Tails

Drop frozen tails into boiling, salted water to cover. Bring water back to boiling; reduce heat and simmer 20 minutes for tails under 10 ounces; 30 minutes for larger ones. Drain lobster tails; rinse under stream of cold water till cool enough to handle.

Serve hot with butter as main course or remove meat for creamed dishes, casseroles, chilled salads, appetizers.

Steamed Clams

Thoroughly scrub 2 dozen clams in shell. Place in kettle with 1 cup hot water; cover tightly and cook over moderate heat just till shells open, about 10 minutes. Serve with melted butter. Makes 4 to 6 servings.

Broil rock-lobster tails with the butterfly cut—easy eating!

To butterfly: Partially thaw frozen lobster tails. Snip through center of hard top shell with kitchen scissors. With sharp knife cut through meat but *not through under shell*. Spread open— now meat is on top. Place on broiler rack, shell down. No turning! (Protect tail "fans" by covering with foil.) Brush the meat well with melted butter—dash in few drops Tabasco.

Broil 4 to 5 inches from heat 10 to 20 minutes for tails under 8 ounces; 15 to 25 minutes for larger ones. Brush often with butter while cooking. Lobster is done when you can flake it with fork. Loosen meat in kitchen: Insert fork between shell and meat, lift to give lobster built-up look. Brush with butter and dash with paprika. See broiled rock-lobster tails on cover.

Friday Banquet Pie—
really fit for a banquet

You'll have to try it yourself to find out how delicious this is! Flaked salmon or tuna bakes in an onion- and basil-flavored custard, sports wedge crust of pastry. Ladle cool Cucumber Sauce or Tartare Sauce over each oven-hot serving.

Friday Banquet Pie

2 beaten eggs
½ cup milk
1 tablespoon butter, melted
¼ cup chopped onion
2 tablespoons minced parsley
¾ teaspoon basil
¼ teaspoon salt
1 1-pound can (2 cups) salmon, or 2
   6½- or 7-ounce cans tuna
1 stick packaged pastry mix

Combine eggs, milk, butter, onion, parsley, and seasonings. Break salmon in chunks, removing bones and skin. Stir salmon into egg mixture. Pour into well-greased 8-inch pie plate. Prepare pastry mix according to package directions. Roll ⅛ inch thick; cut 8-inch circle, then cut circle in 6 wedges. Arrange atop pie. Bake at 425° about 25 minutes. Serve immediately. Pass chilled Cucumber Sauce or Tartare Sauce to spoon atop hot wedges. Serves 6.

Cucumber Sauce

1 medium cucumber,
   unpared
1 tablespoon grated onion
¼ cup mayonnaise
2 teaspoons vinegar
1 tablespoon minced parsley
½ cup dairy sour cream
Salt
Pepper

Cut cucumber in half lengthwise; scoop out seeds. Grate cucumber (you'll need about 1 cup grated); drain. Combine all ingredients, blend well. Chill. Makes 1½ cups.

Tartare Sauce

Combine 1 cup mayonnaise, 1 teaspoon grated onion, 1 tablespoon minced dill pickle, 1 teaspoon minced parsley, 1 teaspoon chopped pimiento, and dash Tabasco.

Scalloped Oysters, right out of the oven — puffy and moist, crunchy on top! Makes a special but easy-does-it supper dish or accompaniment for roast turkey or chicken.

Fried Oysters or Scallops

Drain oysters or scallops; dry between towels. Roll in enriched flour seasoned with salt and pepper. Dip in beaten egg mixed with water, then into dry bread crumbs.

Fry golden brown in deep, hot fat (375°). Drain on paper towels. Or *oven-fry* oysters: Sprinkle both sides of crumb-coated oysters with salad oil. Bake in shallow pan at 400° about 15 minutes. Serve with Tartare Sauce (recipe page 101).

Super Oyster Stew

    2 tablespoons flour
    1½ teaspoons salt
    Few drops Tabasco sauce
    2 tablespoons water
    1 pint oysters
    1 quart milk, scalded

Combine flour, salt, Tabasco, and water; blend to smooth paste. Stir into oysters and liquor. Simmer over very low heat till edges curl. Then pour into milk. Remove pan from heat; cover and let stand 15 minutes— this mellows the flavor. Reheat stew briefly. Serve piping hot in heated soup plates. Drop in some butter or margarine, dash with paprika. Makes 3 or 4 servings.

Perfect Scalloped Oysters

    1 pint oysters
    2 cups medium-coarse cracker crumbs
    ½ cup butter or margarine, melted
    ½ teaspoon salt
    ¾ cup light cream
    ¼ cup oyster liquor
    ¼ teaspoon Worcestershire sauce

Drain oysters, reserving ¼ cup liquor. Combine crumbs, butter, salt. Spread ⅓ of crumbs in greased 8x1¼-inch round pan. Cover with half the oysters. Sprinkle with pepper. Using another third of the crumbs, spread a second layer; cover with remaining oysters. Sprinkle with pepper.

Combine cream, oyster liquor, Worcestershire sauce. Pour over the oysters. Top with last of crumbs. Bake in moderate oven (350°) about 40 minutes. Makes 4 servings.

Fresh-cooked Shrimp

For 1 pound raw cleaned shrimp (2 pounds in shell), combine 6 cups water, 3 tablespoons salt, 2 tablespoons vinegar, 2 bay leaves, 1 teaspoon mixed pickling spices, and 2 stalks of celery; bring to boiling. Add shrimp. Cover, heat to boiling, then lower heat and simmer till shrimp turn pink, about 5 minutes. Drain. If cooked in shell, peel shrimp; remove vein that runs down back. For appetizer, chill; serve with Sea-food Cocktail Sauce. Makes 4 or 5 servings.

French-fried Shrimp

    1 cup enriched flour
    ½ teaspoon sugar
    ½ teaspoon salt
    1 cup ice water
    1 egg
    2 tablespoons salad oil
    1 pound raw cleaned shrimp (2 pounds
      in shell)*

Combine ingredients, except shrimp; beat well. Dry shrimp thoroughly and remove black vein. Dip in batter; fry in deep, hot fat (375°) till golden brown. Drain on paper towels. Serve immediately with Tartare Sauce (page 101) or Sea-food Cocktail Sauce (page 138). Makes 6 servings.

*If you use in-the-shell shrimp, peel, leaving last section and tail of shrimp intact. Cut slit through center back without severing ends; remove black vein.

Fried Fish

Wash cleaned fresh- or salt-water fish and dry thoroughly. Dip in beaten egg mixed with water, then in bread crumbs, seasoned enriched flour, or corn meal.

Brown fish in ¼ inch hot fat or salad oil on one side; turn and brown other side.

Small fish may be fried whole. Larger fish are boned and cut in steaks or fillets.

Baked Fish Fillets

2 pounds fish fillets, fresh or frozen
¼ teaspoon paprika
3 tablespoons lemon juice
2 tablespoons butter or margarine
2 tablespoons enriched flour
Salt and pepper
1 tablespoon dry mustard
1 cup milk
½ cup buttered bread crumbs
1 tablespoon minced parsley

Cut fillets in serving pieces. Place in greased shallow baking dish; sprinkle with paprika, lemon juice, and salt and pepper.

Make white sauce of butter, flour, seasonings, and milk; pour over fillets. Sprinkle with crumbs and parsley. Bake in moderate oven (350°) 35 minutes. Makes 6 servings.

Salmon or Tuna Ring—expertly seasoned! Loaf bakes in a ring mold for pretty-at-the-table look. Center with a bowl of Olive-Almond Sauce and serve with lemon wedges.

Stuffed Fillet Roll-ups

¼ cup chopped onion
¼ cup butter or margarine
4 cups soft bread crumbs
1 teaspoon poultry seasoning
1 cup mayonnaise or salad dressing
1 1-pound package frozen haddock
   fillets

Cook onion in butter till tender. Stir in crumbs, poultry seasoning, and salt and pepper. Blend in ½ cup of the mayonnaise.

Cut fillets in 4 uniform strips, about 1½x 8 inches. Spread each with bread stuffing; roll up, jelly-roll fashion. Place in greased custard cups. Set cups in shallow pan. Bake in moderate oven (350°) about 20 minutes. Spread with rest of mayonnaise. Bake 20 minutes more. Makes 4 servings.

Salmon Steaks

Place six 1-inch salmon steaks in greased shallow baking pan. Melt ⅓ cup butter; add ½ teaspoon salt, ¼ teaspoon paprika, 1 teaspoon Worcestershire sauce; brush over salmon. Sprinkle each steak with 1 teaspoon grated onion. Bake at 350° about 25 to 30 minutes. Serve with Tartare Sauce.

Salmon or Tuna Ring

1 1-pound can (2 cups) red salmon or
   two 6½- or 7-ounce cans tuna,
   drained and flaked
1 cup fine dry bread crumbs
½ cup chopped celery
¼ cup chopped green pepper
2 tablespoons minced onion
1 tablespoon lemon juice
1 cup evaporated milk
1 beaten egg

Combine the salmon, crumbs, vegetables, and lemon juice. Combine milk and egg; add to salmon mixture, mixing gently. Turn into well-greased 5-cup ring mold. Bake in moderate oven (350°) about 30 to 35 minutes. Invert on warm platter and serve with Olive-Almond Sauce. Makes 6 servings.

Olive-Almond Sauce: Combine ¼ cup mayonnaise, 1 tablespoon enriched flour, and ¼ teaspoon salt; blend till smooth. Measure ⅔ cup evaporated milk, and add water to make 1¼ cups; slowly add to mayonnaise mixture. Cook and stir till thick. Add ¼ cup sliced stuffed green olives and ¼ cup chopped salted almonds.

Herb-baked Fish

1 pound frozen haddock, halibut, or cod
1 tablespoon butter or margarine
1 teaspoon salt
½ teaspoon garlic salt
½ teaspoon monosodium glutamate
¼ teaspoon oregano
¼ teaspoon thyme
Dash pepper
1 small bay leaf
½ cup thinly sliced onion, separated
    into rings
½ to ¾ cup light cream

Place frozen fish in 10x6x1½-inch baking dish; dot with butter and sprinkle with the seasonings. Add bay leaf. Arrange onion rings over top of fish and pour cream over all. Bake uncovered in moderate oven (350°) about 40 minutes. Makes 4 servings.

Creole Fillets

1 cup chopped onion
1 cup chopped green pepper
1 clove garlic, minced
2 1-pound cans (4 cups) tomatoes
1 or 2 bay leaves
1½ teaspoons salt
2 pounds frozen halibut fillets

Cook onion, green pepper, and garlic in 3 tablespoons hot fat till tender. Add tomatoes, bay leaf, salt, and dash cayenne; simmer 30 minutes. Place frozen fish in 11½x 7½x1½-inch baking dish. Sprinkle with 1 teaspoon salt and ¼ teaspoon pepper. Pour tomato mixture over fish. Bake in moderate oven (350°) about 45 minutes, or till tender. Makes 6 to 8 servings.

Oven-fried Fish

1 tablespoon salt
½ cup evaporated milk
½ cup water
2 pounds boned fish fillets or steaks
1 cup slightly crushed corn flakes

Dissolve salt in combined milk and water; dip fish in the milk, then roll in corn flakes. Bake on greased cooky sheet at 500° about 15 minutes. Makes 6 servings. Serve with *Caper Sauce:* To one cup mayonnaise, add ¼ cup drained chopped sour pickles, 1 tablespoon drained chopped capers, 1½ teaspoons each prepared mustard and chopped parsley. Makes about 1¼ cups.

Poached Lake Trout

1 3- to 4-pound dressed lake trout
½ cup milk
½ cup water
4 slices lemon
½ teaspoon allspice
½ teaspoon salt
1 recipe Golden Sauce

Place fish in skillet. Add combined milk, water, lemon slices, allspice, and salt. Cover and cook over low heat 20 minutes or till just tender. Carefully remove trout to hot platter. Trim with parsley and serve with Golden Sauce. Makes 6 servings.

Golden Sauce: Melt ¼ cup butter or margarine; blend in ¼ cup enriched flour. Gradually add 2 cups milk; cook and stir till thick. Add 1½ tablespoons lemon juice and 2 hard-cooked eggs, chopped.

Tuna 'n Rice Souffle

1 can condensed cream of mushroom
    soup
1 6½- or 7-ounce can (1 cup) tuna,
    drained
1 cup cooked rice
¼ cup chopped pimiento
2 tablespoons chopped parsley
4 eggs, separated

Heat and stir soup over low heat; add next 4 ingredients and heat. Beat egg whites till stiff. Beat egg yolks till thick and lemon-colored; gradually stir in tuna mixture. Fold into egg whites. Pour into ungreased 2-quart casserole. Bake in moderate oven (350°) 30 to 35 minutes or till mixture is set in center. Serve at once with lemon wedges. Makes 6 servings.

Tuna Salad Bake

1 can condensed cream of chicken soup
1 6½-, 7-, or 9¼-ounce can tuna
1 cup diced celery
¼ cup finely chopped onion
½ cup salad dressing or mayonnaise
½ teaspoon salt
¼ teaspoon pepper
3 hard-cooked eggs, sliced
1 cup crushed potato chips

Mix soup, drained tuna, celery, onion, salad dressing, and seasonings; fold in egg slices. Pile lightly into 1½-quart casserole. Sprinkle with crushed chips. Bake in hot oven (400°) 25 minutes. Serves 6.

Serve elegant Avocado Pontchartrain with Shrimp Remoulade as done by the famous New Orleans Pontchartrain Hotel. Fresh plump shrimp take on a luscious Remoulade blend.

Avocado Pontchartrain with Shrimp Remoulade

In a small bowl, combine ¼ cup tarragon vinegar, 2 tablespoons horseradish mustard, 1 tablespoon catsup, 1½ teaspoons paprika, ½ teaspoon salt, and ¼ teaspoon cayenne pepper. Slowly add ½ cup salad oil, beating constantly. Stir in ¼ cup minced celery, and ¼ cup minced green onions and tops. Pour Remoulade Sauce over 2 pounds shrimp, cleaned and cooked. Let shrimp marinate in refrigerator for 4 to 5 hours.

Halve and peel 4 medium avocados. Lift shrimp out of sauce and arrange 5 to 6 shrimp on each avocado half.

If desired, serve with arranged cooked chilled asparagus spears, carrot strips, sliced cooked chilled beets, and sliced hard-cooked eggs. Pass additional Remoulade Sauce or French Dressing. Makes 8 servings.

Sea-food Pilaf

¾ cup uncooked long-grain rice
2 tablespoons butter or margarine

• • •

1 3-ounce can (⅔ cup) broiled sliced mushrooms
1 10½-ounce can condensed chicken-rice soup
1 7½-ounce can crab meat, drained and flaked
1 4½- or 5-ounce can shrimp, drained
¼ cup dry sherry
1 tablespoon instant minced onion

In skillet, brown rice in butter, about 5 minutes. Add mushrooms (and liquid) and remaining ingredients. Turn into 1½-quart casserole. Bake covered in moderate oven (350°) for 55 minutes. Fluff with fork. Bake uncovered 5 minutes longer. Serves 6.

Specialties to make you famous

Shrimp de Jonghe

You'll treasure this recipe for buffet parties—simple to make and so good!—

1 cup butter, melted
2 to 4 cloves garlic, minced
⅓ cup chopped parsley
½ teaspoon paprika
Dash cayenne
⅔ cup cooking sherry

• • •

2 cups soft bread crumbs

• • •

5 to 6 cups cleaned cooked shrimp (4 pounds in shell)

To melted butter, add garlic, parsley, paprika, cayenne, and cooking sherry; mix. Add bread crumbs; toss. Place shrimp in 11x 7x1½-inch baking dish. Spoon the butter mixture over. Bake in slow oven (325°) 20 to 25 minutes, or till crumbs brown. Sprinkle with additional chopped parsley before serving. Makes 6 to 8 servings.

Shrimp de Jonghe (say "Jonghe" like "wrong")

Tuna Tetrazzini

½ cup chopped onion
1 tablespoon fat
1 can condensed cream of mushroom soup
1 6-ounce can (⅔ cup) evaporated milk or ⅔ cup light cream
⅓ cup grated Parmesan cheese
1 6½-, 7-, or 9¼-ounce can tuna, drained
1 3-ounce can (⅔ cup) broiled sliced mushrooms, drained
½ cup chopped ripe olives
2 tablespoons minced parsley
2 teaspoons lemon juice
6 ounces noodles, cooked and drained

Cook onion in hot fat till tender but not brown. Add soup, evaporated milk, and cheese; heat and stir. Break tuna in chunks; add with remaining ingredients. Pour into greased 2-quart casserole.

Sprinkle with additional Parmesan cheese and paprika. Bake in moderate oven (375°) 20 to 25 minutes. Top with ripe olives. Makes 6 servings.

Company Tuna Bake

1 3-ounce package cream cheese
1 can condensed cream of mushroom soup
1 6½-, 7-, or 9¼-ounce can tuna, drained and flaked
1½ tablespoons chopped pimiento
1 tablespoon chopped onion
1 tablespoon prepared mustard
¼ cup milk
½ 6-ounce package (1 cup) 7-minute macaroni, cooked and drained

• • •

½ cup dry medium bread crumbs
2 tablespoons butter or margarine, melted

Soften cream cheese; blend in soup using electric or rotary beater. Stir in tuna, pimiento, onion, mustard, milk, and macaroni. Spoon into 1½-quart casserole. Mix crumbs and butter; sprinkle over top.

Bake in moderate oven (375°) 20 to 25 minutes, or till heated thoroughly. Garnish with pimiento flower and parsley, if desired. Makes 4 or 5 servings.

← # 15-minute Tuna Curry

⅓ cup chopped onion
¼ cup chopped green pepper
1 clove garlic, minced
1 cup dairy sour cream
1 teaspoon curry powder
Salt and pepper
1 6½-, 7-, or 9¼-ounce can tuna

Cook onion, green pepper, and garlic in 2 tablespoons butter till tender but not brown. Stir in sour cream and seasonings. Drain tuna and break in bite-size pieces; add. Heat slowly stirring often, just till hot. Serve over hot rice dotted with raisins.

Makes 4 servings.

Trader Vic's Shrimp Foo Yong

Foo yong means omelet, and you can have shrimp or any kind you want: Crab meat, pork, lobster, or chicken—cooked or canned—

¾ cup cooked tiny shrimp or chopped cooked sea food
1 cup bean sprouts
1 tablespoon chopped green onions
1 tablespoon chopped bamboo shoots
1 tablespoon finely chopped water chestnuts
3 mushrooms, chopped
1 teaspoon monosodium glutamate
Salt
4 eggs

Combine all ingredients, adding eggs last. Mix well. Put plenty of cooking oil (2 tablespoons) in hot skillet or on a hot griddle, and drop a liberal amount of the egg mixture (about ⅓ cup) to form small cakes. Fry them over high heat into thick cakes, turning once, until cooked and delicately browned. Pile several together for a serving and pour over them *Foo Yong Sauce:*

1 cup chicken broth
¼ teaspoon sugar
2 tablespoons soy sauce
2 teaspoons monosodium glutamate
1 tablespoon cornstarch
¼ cup cold water

Heat broth in a small pan; add rest of ingredients except cornstarch and water. Combine cornstarch and cold water, add to sauce and cook, stirring constantly, till mixture thickens to the consistency of gravy. Season with salt to taste. Makes 6 cakes.

Crab-stuffed Artichokes

2 6½-ounce cans (2 cups) crab meat
1 cup cubed process Swiss cheese
⅓ cup chopped green pepper
¼ cup finely chopped onion
½ cup mayonnaise or salad dressing
2 teaspoons lemon juice
5 cooked medium artichokes

Drain crab meat; break in chunks; toss with cheese, green pepper, onion, and 1 teaspoon salt. Add mayonnaise and lemon juice to crab mixture; toss lightly. Remove small center leaves and choke of each artichoke, leaving a cup. Fill artichokes with crab salad; place in large casserole. Pour hot water around artichokes to depth of 1 inch. Cover; bake at 375° about 35 minutes.

Sea-food Turnovers

1 can condensed cream of mushroom soup
1 7¾-ounce can lobster meat or 1 6½-ounce can crab meat, flaked
¼ cup mayonnaise or salad dressing
½ teaspoon Worcestershire sauce
¼ teaspoon monosodium glutamate
1 package pastry mix

Combine ½ cup of the soup (reserve remainder) with sea food, mayonnaise, and seasonings. Prepare pastry according to package directions; roll in four 6-inch circles. Place ¼ of the filling on half of each circle; fold to form turnovers and seal edges with fork. Prick top. Place on ungreased baking sheet. Bake at 450° 15 to 20 minutes. Serve hot with sauce of reserved soup, heated with 2 tablespoons milk.

When he brings home game, cook it right

Fried Rabbit or Squirrel

Cut dressed rabbit or squirrel in serving pieces: Disjoint legs at body and second joints; split down center back and through breast, cutting each half in two. (Many folks like to soak meat in salted water a few hours before cooking; drain.) Dip meat in melted butter, then in crushed corn flakes. Brown in hot fat; reduce heat; cook slowly about 1 hour. If animal is of uncertain age, add small amount hot water; cover and cook slowly about 1½ hours.

Hasenpfeffer

1 2½- to 3-pound dressed rabbit,
   cut in serving pieces
2 to 3 cups vinegar
2 to 3 cups water
½ cup sugar
1 medium onion, sliced
2 teaspoons salt
¼ teaspoon pepper
1 teaspoon pickling spices

Cover rabbit with equal amounts vinegar and water; add sugar, onion, seasonings, and spices. Let stand in refrigerator 2 days.

Remove rabbit; dry; dip pieces in flour and brown in hot fat. Gradually add 1 cup of the vinegar water; cover and simmer about 1 hour or till tender. Remove meat to hot platter. Thicken liquid with enriched flour for gravy. Makes 4 servings.

Antelope

Antelope can be used in most recipes for venison. Chef's tip: Moist heat is usually best for cooking antelope—it's leaner.

Venison

Venison includes any game from the deer family. The venison most commonly eaten is deer. Elk is next, then moose. Venison from a freshly killed animal should age in a cool place 1 to 2 weeks, according to taste. For best flavor, trim off all fat. You may lard the meat with salt pork or bacon for cooking.

Cook venison same as beef. Tender cuts— roasts, rib and loin chops, or steaks from the leg—are cooked by dry heat: broiling or roasting. Many folks like venison fixed this way rare. Or you may prefer it well done. Before roasting or broiling, venison may be chilled overnight in Beef Marinade (page 24)—turn meat several times.

Less-tender cuts or meat from animals of uncertain age are cooked slowly by moist heat, usually braised, till well done. Venison makes wonderful pot roast—see recipes for Beef Pot Roast or Sauerbraten (page 28). Or have meatman grind less-tender meat with a little salt pork for burgers.

Roast Venison

Choose a tender 3- to 5-pound loin, round, or shoulder roast. Season; place on rack in shallow roasting pan. Top with strips of bacon. Roast at 325° till medium-well done or 30 to 35 minutes *per pound*. During roasting, meat may be brushed frequently with Warren's Barbecue Sauce.

Broiled Venison Steaks

4 ½-inch venison steaks from leg, or
   rib or loin chops from *young* animal
2 tablespoons salad oil
¼ cup butter or margarine, melted
1 tablespoon onion juice

Brush steaks with salad oil; let stand 15 minutes. Broil 3 inches from heat 7 to 10 minutes on each side. Combine butter, onion juice, dash of salt; brush on steaks.

Pan-broiled Venison Steaks

Marinate four ½-inch tender venison steaks or chops in 1 cup clear French dressing 30 minutes. Drain. Heat heavy skillet; brown meat on both sides, using a bit of butter if needed. Sprinkle with salt, pepper. Finish cooking over low heat, pouring off any fat. Brush steaks with melted butter.

Roast Pheasant

Roast only young birds—their feet are still gray, the spur is rounded and flexible. The last big wing feather has pointed tip.

Clean bird. Salt inside and fill cavity loosely with Herb Stuffing (page 38). Truss bird and place breast up on rack in shallow roasting pan. Place bacon slices over breast. Roast in slow to moderate oven (325° to 350°) 1½ hours or till tender.

Smothered Pheasant

Good with grouse or quail, too. Of course, smaller birds cook in less time—

Clean pheasant and cut in serving pieces. Roll in seasoned flour. In Dutch oven, brown meat slowly on both sides in ½ cup hot fat, turning once. Top with 2 cups sliced onions; pour over 1 cup water, milk, or light cream. Cover tightly and cook top of range over low heat or bake in slow oven (325°) till tender, about 1 hour. Serve with gravy made from drippings. Serves 3 or 4.

Quail, Grouse, Partridge, and Woodcock

These birds may be cooked in the same way. Recipe below for Quail in Sour Cream is as delicious with one of the other birds— just allow more cooking time for larger size.

Quail in Sour Cream

6 quail, about ½ pound each, cleaned and dressed
6 thin slices bacon or salt pork
• • •
12 juniper berries (optional)
1 cup boiling water
• • •
2 cups dairy sour cream
1 tablespoon lemon juice
Few drops Tabasco sauce
Dash salt
Dash pepper

Wrap each bird in slice of bacon; fasten with toothpicks. Crush juniper berries in Dutch oven; place birds atop and pour over boiling water. Cover and simmer 35 minutes or till birds are tender. Combine sour cream, lemon juice, Tabasco sauce, salt, and pepper; pour over quail and heat sauce just through. Makes 6 servings.

Roast Wild Duck, Goose, or Turkey

Rub inside of bird with salt. Stuff loosely with quartered onions and apples. Truss bird if large and place breast up on rack in shallow roasting pan. Brush with salad oil, melted butter or margarine, or lay bacon slices over breast. If bird is of uncertain age, you may want to pour about 1 cup boiling water in pan. Roast in moderate oven (350°) 40 to 45 minutes *per pound* or till bird is tender. Baste frequently with pan drippings. Discard stuffing and serve. Allow 1 to 1½ pounds per person.

Note: If duck or goose has had a fish diet or bird is not so young, stuff loosely with pared carrot or quartered potato and pre-cook in simmering water about 10 minutes. Then remove the stuffing, and stuff and roast as in above recipe.

Hunter's Duck

If you're among those who prefer the real gamy flavor, roast tender young ducks, whole (1½ to 2 pounds), in very hot oven (450°) for 40 to 45 minutes or just long enough to acquire a crispy brown crust.

Wild Duck or Goose with Sauerkraut

1 wild duck or goose, cleaned
1 lemon
• • •
1 1-pound can (2 cups) sauerkraut
½ teaspoon celery seed
1 teaspoon sugar
Dash pepper
• • •
1 cup boiling water
¾ cup cooking sherry

Rub bird, inside and out, with cut side of lemon, squeezing juice occasionally. Combine sauerkraut, celery seed, sugar, and pepper; stuff bird loosely and truss.

Place breast up on rack in shallow roasting pan; pour in boiling water. Cover and roast in moderate oven (350°) 40 to 45 minutes per pound or till nearly done. Remove cover and drain liquid from pan. Roast uncovered till done, about 30 more minutes, basting frequently with the cooking sherry.

Serve on heated platter; garnish with orange slices and fluffs of parsley.

Note: Another time, stuff bird with your favorite wild-rice stuffing.

Baby Cream Puffs—luscious little appetizers stuffed with deviled ham or your favorite ham, chicken, or crab-meat salad. Puffs are made in miniature from your favorite recipe. For extra crispness split baked puffs almost in half. Turn off heat; put puffs back in oven 10 minutes.

Appetizer Ham Ball

2 4½-ounce cans deviled ham
3 tablespoons chopped stuffed olives
1 tablespoon prepared mustard
Tabasco sauce to taste
1 3-ounce package cream cheese
2 teaspoons milk

Blend deviled ham, olives, mustard, and Tabasco. Form in ball on serving dish. Chill. Soften cream cheese with milk, and frost ball. Keep chilled; remove from refrigerator 15 minutes before serving time. Serve with assorted crackers.

Water-chestnut Hors d'Oeuvres

1 5-ounce can (⅔ cup) whole water chestnuts, drained
¼ cup soy sauce
2 tablespoons sugar
3 slices bacon

Let water chestnuts stand in soy sauce about 30 minutes. Roll each in sugar. Cut bacon in half lengthwise, then crosswise. Wrap each water chestnut with piece of bacon; anchor with toothpick. Place on rack in shallow baking pan; bake at 400° about 20 minutes. Drain on paper towels. Serve hot.

For meal starters or

Beef Fondue

Guests cook their own tenderloin cubes—

1½ pounds trimmed beef tenderloin, cut in ¾-inch cubes (3 cups)
Salad oil

• • •

Garlic Butter
Creamy Horseradish Sauce
Tomato Steak Sauce
Anchovy Butter

Pour salad oil in a deep chafing dish to depth of about 1½ inches. Place over direct heat on range and bring to 425° or just below smoking point. Then take to table and place over alcohol burner or canned heat. Have beef cubes at room temperature in serving bowl. Set out small bowls of several or all of the special butters and sauces. Each guest spears beef cube with fork, then holds it in hot oil until cooked to desired doneness. He then dips it in a sauce on his plate. (When salad oil cools so meat no longer cooks briskly, heat oil again on range. Treat hot oil with respect—be ever so careful in moving the pan.)

Garlic Butter: Whip ½ cup softened butter till fluffy. Stir in 1 clove garlic, minced. If fixed ahead, chill; let come to room temperature before serving. Makes ½ cup.

Creamy Horseradish Sauce: Combine 1 cup dairy sour cream, 3 tablespoons drained prepared horseradish, ¼ teaspoon salt, and dash paprika. Chill. Makes 1¼ cups.

Tomato Steak Sauce: Mix one 8-ounce can (1 cup) seasoned tomato sauce, ⅓ cup bottled steak sauce, 2 tablespoons brown sugar, and 2 tablespoons salad oil. Heat to boiling. Serve hot. Makes 1½ cups.

Anchovy Butter: Drain one 2-ounce can anchovy fillets; place in blender or mixer with ½ cup soft butter or margarine, 2 tablespoons olive or salad oil, ½ teaspoon paprika, and ⅛ teaspoon freshly ground pepper. Beat smooth. If fixed ahead, chill; let come to room temperature; serve. Makes 1 cup.

any time—appetizers, snacks

Caviar Canapes

Spread chilled caviar—black or red—on rounds of melba toast. Dash with a few drops of lemon juice or Tabasco sauce. Or sprinkle lightly with finely chopped onion or egg white or sieved egg yolk.

Curried Chicken Dip

In blender, combine one 5-ounce can boned chicken, one 3-ounce can broiled chopped mushrooms, drained, 1 cup dairy sour cream, and 2 to 3 teaspoons curry powder. Switch blender on and off, blending mixture till smooth; chill. At serving time, stir in ½ cup finely chopped cashews. Serve with crisp relishes, assorted crackers, or chips.

Smoked Turkey

Smoked turkey is wonderful as is served in thin slices. Or spread melba-toast rounds with softened cream cheese and top with the turkey sliced paper thin. Dash with pepper.

Smoked Salmon

Serve thin slices of smoked salmon with buttered rounds of salty ice-box rye bread.

Easy entertaining!

Sizzling Steak Canapes—sturdy tidbits for the crowd. While guests watch, Dad carves meat, flips each slice on a thin round of salty rye.

Use strip sirloin steak—or you may know it as New York or Kansas City cut. (Watch for packaged frozen strip steak at frozen-foods counter.) Or use whole beef tenderloin.

Have steak cut 1½ to 2 inches thick. Place in broiler so top of steak is 2 to 4 inches from heat. Broil one side; season; turn with tongs and broil other side to doneness you like. Season. Slice thin and serve hot.

Cold Marinated Beef Slices

A specialty at Chicago's Stock Yard Inn

Cut ½ pound cooked sirloin steak or beef roast in thin strips. Thinly slice 1 small onion and separate in rings. Combine beef and onion with ¾ teaspoon salt and dash pepper. Sprinkle with 1½ tablespoons lemon juice. Stir in 1 cup dairy sour cream; chill. Serve in lettuce-lined dishes with lemon wedges. Trim with pimiento and green pepper strips. Makes 6 servings.

Lobster-ettes for snacktime!

Serve in their pretty shells

Chicken Canapes

1 5-ounce can chicken spread
2 teaspoons mayonnaise or salad dressing
½ cup chopped salted almonds, toasted
2 tablespoons sweet-pickle relish

• • •

Canned jellied cranberry sauce

Combine first four ingredients. Spread on crackers. Trim with tiny cranberry-sauce cutouts. Makes about ¾ cup spread.

Lobster-ettes

Tiny frozen lobster tails that weigh only 1 to 2 ounces apiece come from Denmark. Each makes two or three bites. They are orange-colored, change to red when cooked. Slightly larger lobster tails—2 to 4 ounces—come from South Africa, Australia, or New Zealand and may be fixed same way, but need a bit longer cooking time because of their size.

To broil: Thaw, then butterfly: With sharp knife, cut lengthwise along back, but not through undershell. Spread open in butterfly fashion; remove sand vein. Brush meat with melted butter or margarine (add a drop or so of Tabasco if you like). Place shell down on broiler-pan rack. Broil 3 inches from heat about 7 minutes for 1- to 2-ouncers (longer for larger ones), brushing frequently with melted butter. Sprinkle with paprika and serve immediately.

To simmer: Thaw and cut butterfly fashion as for broiling. Cook as you would shrimp, in well-salted water seasoned with pickling spices. Simmer, *don't boil*, about 5 minutes for 1- to 2-ouncers (longer for the larger ones). Serve immediately.

How to serve: Nestle the pretty steaming-hot lobster tails (in shells) on water cress. Offer lemon wedges and bowls of drawn butter, cocktail and tartare sauces.

Best-ever nibbling—midget burgers and frank slices

←

Midget Burgers. Toast 10 slices bread on one side; cut four 1½-inch rounds from each. Butter untoasted sides. Mix 1 pound of ground beef, 1 tablespoon Worcestershire, 1 teaspoon salt. Shape in 40 tiny balls; place one on buttered side of each round. Make indentation in center of balls. Broil 4 inches from heat 5 to 6 minutes. Fill with chili sauce.

→

Sweet-'n-sour Cocktail Wieners. Mix one 6-ounce jar (¾ cup) prepared mustard and one 10-ounce jar (1 cup) currant jelly in chafing dish or electric skillet, using low heat. Diagonally slice 1 pound (8 to 10) frankfurters; add to sauce and heat till cooked through.

Jiffy Pizza Snacks

Snip 10 refrigerated biscuits in two with scissors. Roll each in ball; place on baking sheet. With floured bottom of custard cup, flatten to 2½-inch circles, leaving rim. Mix ⅓ cup canned tomato paste, 1 tablespoon crushed oregano, and 1 clove garlic, minced. Quickly spread on the biscuit rounds. Slice brown-and-serve sausages from an 8-ounce package; arrange slices on biscuits. Sprinkle with ¾ cup shredded sharp process cheese and ¼ cup grated Parmesan. Bake at 425° about 10 minutes or till done.

Pickled Shrimp

   2½ pounds shrimp in shell
   ½ cup celery tops
   ¼ cup mixed pickling spices
   3½ teaspoons salt
   2 cups sliced onion
   7 or 8 bay leaves

Cover shrimp with boiling water; add celery, spices, salt. Cover; simmer 5 minutes. Drain; cool. Peel shrimp; devein. Alternate shrimp and onion in shallow dish. Add bay leaves. Marinate 24 hours in *Pickling Marinade:* Mix 1¼ cups salad oil, ¾ cup white vinegar, 3 tablespoons capers and juice, 2½ teaspoons celery seed, 1½ teaspoons salt, and dash Tabasco sauce. Mix well. Pour over shrimp. Cover and chill.

Clam Cocktail Dunk

   2 3-ounce packages cream cheese, softened
   2 teaspoons lemon juice
   2 teaspoons grated onion
      or 3 drops onion juice
   1 teaspoon Worcestershire sauce
   3 or 4 drops Tabasco sauce
   ¼ teaspoon salt
   1 7- or 7½-ounce can (about 1 cup) minced clams, chilled and drained
   1 tablespoon minced parsley

Combine cream cheese, lemon juice, onion, Worcestershire, Tabasco, and salt. Beat with electric or rotary beater till fluffy. Stir in clams and parsley. Serve with crackers, chips, or crisp relishes. Makes 1½ cups.

Deviled Dip

   1 5-ounce jar pimento-cheese spread
   1 4½-ounce can deviled ham
   ½ cup mayonnaise or salad dressing
   2 tablespoons minced parsley
   1 tablespoon minced onion
   4 drops Tabasco sauce
   Dash monosodium glutamate

With electric or rotary beater, thoroughly combine cheese spread, deviled ham, mayonnaise, parsley, onion, and seasonings. Chill. Makes about 1⅓ cups. Serve with assorted crackers and potato chips.

Liver cheese or liver sausage with a flair—as is or in a dip

Liver cheese goes to a party! Peel white jacket from 1-pound loaf of liver cheese; smooth the surface. Peg a row of stuffed green or black olives on cocktail picks along sides. Have spreaders ready, and plenty of crackers.

Or whip up a dip from liver sausage. This one's nice and spicy. *Snacktime Dip:* Mix ½ pound liver sausage, 3 tablespoons chopped sweet or dill pickle, ¼ cup chopped onion, ¼ cup salad dressing, 2 teaspoons prepared mustard, ¾ teaspoon Worcestershire, and ⅛ to ¼ teaspoon Tabasco sauce. Add salt to taste; chill. Remove from refrigerator ½ hour before serving. Pass with potato chips or crackers.

No need to brown these drumsticks. Corn 'n Chicken Scallop goes straight to the oven.

Casseroles,

Cheddar Turkey Casserole

There's a quick cheese soup sauce beneath, crushed cheese crackers atop—

1 cup packaged precooked rice
2 tablespoons instant minced onion
½ 10-ounce package frozen green peas, thawed and broken apart (about 1 cup)*
4 to 6 slices cooked turkey *or* 2 cups diced cooked turkey

. . .

1 11-ounce can condensed Cheddar cheese soup
1 cup milk
1 cup finely crushed rich round cheese crackers
3 tablespoons butter or margarine, melted

Prepare rice according to package directions, *adding the instant minced onion to the boiling water.* Fluff cooked rice with a fork and spread in a greased 10x6x1½-inch baking dish. Sprinkle with peas, then cover with turkey. Blend soup and milk; pour evenly over the turkey. Combine crumbs and butter; sprinkle over casserole. Bake in moderate oven (350°) for 35 minutes or till heated through. Makes 4 to 6 servings.

*Or use 1 cup drained canned peas.

Corn 'n Chicken Scallop

In a large shallow casserole (or a 13x9x2-inch baking dish), thoroughly combine one 1-pound can cream-style corn, 1 cup milk, 1 egg, and 1 tablespoon instant-type flour. Snip in about 6 green onions and tops; stir to distribute onions.

Generously sprinkle 6 to 8 chicken drumsticks with paprika; arrange drumsticks over corn. Dash with seasoned salt; crumble about 30 saltines over all; dot with chunks of butter or margarine (about ½ stick).

Bake in a moderate oven (350°) for 1 hour or till chicken is tender. Drain one 3-ounce can (⅔ cup) broiled sliced mushrooms; place in center of casserole. Return to oven a few minutes to heat through. If desired, garnish with parsley and serve with a crisp green salad. Makes 3 to 4 servings.

Big-Biscuit Hamburger Bake

Cook 1 pound ground beef and ½ cup chopped onion till meat is brown; drain off excess fat. Stir in one 10½-ounce can condensed cream of vegetable soup, ½ teaspoon crushed oregano, and dash freshly ground pepper; heat to bubbling. Turn into an 8¼x1¾-inch round ovenware cake dish.

Top with *Big Biscuit:* Add ½ cup milk, all at once, to 1 cup packaged biscuit mix. Stir with fork into a soft dough; beat 15 strokes. Spread over *hot* meat mixture. Bake in a very hot oven (450°) for 15 minutes or till browned. Spread biscuit with ½ cup dairy sour cream. Sprinkle with ½ cup shredded Parmesan cheese, then snipped parsley. Bake 2 minutes longer. Makes 6 servings.

one-dish meals

Beef and Noodle Casserole

1 box noodles with sour-cream-
   and-cheese sauce mix
1 pound ground beef
½ cup chopped onion
1 10½-ounce can condensed cream of
   mushroom soup
½ cup milk
2 tablespoons chopped canned
   pimiento
¼ teaspoon thyme, crushed
Dash pepper

     • • •

1 cup soft bread crumbs
2 tablespoons melted butter or
   margarine
½ cup shredded sharp Cheddar cheese

Prepare the noodles with sauce mix according to label directions. Brown meat and onion. Stir in soup, milk, pimiento, and seasonings; add noodle mixture.

Turn into 10x6x1½-inch baking dish. Sprinkle with mixture of bread crumbs and butter or margarine. Bake in moderate oven (350°) for 30 minutes. Sprinkle with cheese; bake 5 minutes. Makes 6 servings.

Chicken-Chow Bake

Oriental dinner that's a snap—

2 cups diced cooked or canned
   chicken
1 10½-ounce can condensed cream of
   mushroom soup
1 9-ounce can (1 cup) pineapple
   tidbits
1 tablespoon soy sauce
1 cup celery slices
2 tablespoons chopped green onions
1 3-ounce can (2½ cups) chow-mein
   noodles

Combine diced chicken, soup, pineapple, soy sauce, celery, and chopped green onions; mix well. Gently fold in *1 cup of the noodles.* Turn into 8x8x2-inch baking dish. Sprinkle with remaining noodles. Bake in moderate oven (350°) for 50 minutes or till hot. Makes 4 to 6 servings. Pass soy sauce.

Shrimp Buffet Casserole

Cook ½ cup chopped green pepper and ½ cup chopped onion in 2 tablespoons butter or margarine till tender but not brown. Stir in 3 cups cleaned cooked or canned shrimp, 1 tablespoon lemon juice, 2 cups cooked rice, one 10½-ounce can condensed tomato soup, ¾ cup light cream, ¼ cup cooking sherry, ¾ teaspoon salt, and ¼ teaspoon nutmeg. Pour into 2-quart casserole. Bake at 350° for 30 minutes. Serves 6 to 8.

Frank-'n-Noodle Supper

Combine one No. 2½ can (3½ cups) tomatoes, ½ cup water, 1 envelope spaghetti-sauce mix, 1 cup chopped celery, 1 tablespoon instant minced onion, and 1½ teaspoons sugar. Cut 6 frankfurters in thirds diagonally; brown in 2 tablespoons butter or margarine. Add 4 ounces (3½ cups) medium noodles; pour sauce over, moistening all. Cover; cook over low heat, stirring occasionally, 25 minutes or till done. Sprinkle with ½ cup shredded sharp American cheese. Makes 4 servings.

Lazy Friday Casserole

1¾ cups milk
½ cup cooking sherry
1 can condensed cream of chicken soup
1⅓ cups packaged precooked rice
1 4½-ounce can shrimp, drained and
   split lengthwise
1 5-ounce can lobster, drained and
   cut up
1 7½-ounce can minced clams, drained
1 3-ounce can (⅔ cup) broiled
   sliced mushrooms, drained
1 tablespoon parsley flakes
¼ teaspoon instant minced garlic
¼ cup toasted slivered almonds
2 tablespoons butter or margarine

Stir milk and sherry into soup. Add rice, shrimp, drained lobster, minced clams, mushrooms, parsley flakes, and garlic. Turn into 2-quart casserole. Sprinkle with paprika and almonds; dot with butter. Bake at 350° for 50 minutes. Makes 6 servings.

Garden Chicken Bake

3 tablespoons butter, margarine, or
   chicken fat
3 tablespoons enriched flour
1½ cups chicken broth*

. . .

2 cups cooked chicken cut in pieces
1 cup drained cooked or canned peas
1 3-ounce can (⅔ cup) broiled sliced
   mushrooms, drained
2 cooked medium carrots, cut in thirds
¼ cup chopped onion
2 tablespoons chopped pimiento
1 teaspoon salt

. . .

1 package refrigerated biscuits

Melt butter; blend in flour. Gradually add broth. Cook and stir till thick. Add chicken, vegetables, and salt; heat to bubbling. Pour into 1½-quart casserole.

Prepare *Biscuit Snippets:* Snip 6 refrigerated biscuits in quarters; arrange in ring, rounded side down, on top of *hot* chicken. Bake in hot oven (425°) 8 to 10 minutes or till biscuits are done. (Bake remaining biscuits on baking sheet.) Makes 5 servings.

*Use canned broth or dissolve 2 chicken bouillon cubes in 1½ cups hot water.

Veal Cubes with Dumplings

1½ pounds veal stew meat, cut in
   1-inch cubes
4 cups tomato juice
2 teaspoons salt
1½ teaspoons monosodium glutamate
4 to 6 dashes Tabasco sauce
1 cup diced pared potatoes
½ cup sliced celery
½ cup chopped onion
2 tablespoons minced parsley
1 10-ounce package corn-bread mix

Roll meat in flour. Brown slowly in small amount hot fat in Dutch oven; add tomato juice and seasonings. Cover and simmer (don't boil) 1 hour. Add vegetables; cover and continue cooking about 30 minutes or till vegetables are almost done.

Corn-meal Dumplings: Add parsley to corn-bread mix. *Using only ⅓ cup milk,* prepare batter according to package directions. Drop rounded tablespoons onto hot bubbling stew. (Dumplings will slide off spoon easily if you dip spoon in stew first each time.) Cover tightly and steam (don't lift cover) about 10 minutes or till dumplings are done. Makes 6 servings.

Old-time Potpie

2 pounds beef stew meat, cut in
   1½-inch cubes
1 teaspoon Worcestershire sauce
1 clove garlic
1 medium onion, sliced
1 bay leaf
1 tablespoon salt
1 teaspoon sugar
¼ teaspoon pepper
½ teaspoon paprika
6 small carrots, halved
6 small potatoes, pared and halved
6 small onions

Thoroughly brown meat on all sides in small amount hot fat; add 3 cups boiling water, Worcestershire sauce, garlic, onion, bay leaf, and seasonings. Cover; simmer 2 hours, stirring occasionally. Remove bay leaf and garlic. Add vegetables. Cover and cook about 30 minutes longer. Transfer meat and vegetables to a serving bowl. Thicken liquid as below; pour into the bowl. Top with ring of hot Thimble Rolls. Makes 6 to 8 servings.

To thicken gravy: Skim most of fat from stew liquid. For 2½ cups stock, use these proportions: Put ½ cup cold water into a shaker, add ¼ cup enriched flour. Shake till smooth. Remove stock from heat; slowly stir in flour mixture. Cook, stirring constantly till gravy is bubbling all over. Cook about 5 minutes more, stirring often.

Thimble Rolls

1 package active dry yeast *or* 1 cake
   compressed yeast
¾ cup water
2½ cups packaged biscuit mix
Melted butter or margarine

Soften active dry yeast in *warm* water or compressed yeast in *lukewarm* water. Stir in biscuit mix; beat vigorously, about 3 minutes. Turn out on surface well dusted with biscuit mix. Knead till smooth, about 20 strokes. Roll to slightly less than ½ inch. Cut with floured 1-inch cutter (or center of doughnut cutter). In greased 8x1½-inch round pan, arrange 2 rows of rolls close together around edge. Brush tops with butter; cover with damp cloth; let rise in warm place till double, 30 to 45 minutes. Bake in hot oven (400°) 12 to 15 minutes or till done. (Bake remaining rolls in another pan.) Brush again with butter. Immediately place on top of Old-time Potpie and serve.

Ham-Chicken Bake with Yam Biscuits

Can't beat this Southern-style cooking! In a rush? Skip the biscuit topping —just sprinkle generously with grated Parmesan cheese and bake.

Ham-Chicken Bake

2 cups diced cooked or canned ham
2 cups diced cooked or canned chicken

. . .

¼ cup butter or margarine
¼ cup enriched flour
1 cup chicken broth or 2 chicken bouillon cubes in 1 cup hot water
1 cup light cream
¼ teaspoon salt
Dash pepper
½ cup chopped onion
1 3-ounce can (⅔ cup) broiled sliced mushrooms, drained
1 recipe Yam Biscuits

Place diced ham and chicken in 2-quart casserole. Melt butter; blend in flour. Stir in broth and cream; cook and stir till thick. Add seasonings, onion, mushrooms; pour over ham and chicken. Top *hot* mixture with Yam Biscuits; bake in moderate oven (350°) about 45 minutes. Or instead of Yam Biscuits, pop 6 or 7 hot baked refrigerator biscuits on *baked* casserole. Makes 8 servings.

Yam Biscuits: Combine 1 cup mashed cooked yams, ⅓ cup melted butter, 1 beaten egg. Sift together 1 cup sifted enriched flour, 2 teaspoons baking powder, ½ teaspoon salt; blend into yams. Drop by tablespoons around edge of casserole. Bake as above.

Ground Beef in Sour Cream

1 cup chopped onion
2 tablespoons fat
1 pound ground beef
3 cups medium noodles
3 cups tomato juice
1 teaspoon salt
1½ teaspoons celery salt
Dash pepper
2 teaspoons Worcestershire sauce
¼ to ½ cup chopped green pepper

. . .

1 cup dairy sour cream
1 3-ounce can (⅔ cup) broiled sliced mushrooms, drained

Cook onion in hot fat till tender but not brown. Add beef; brown lightly. Place noodles in layer over meat. Combine tomato juice and seasonings; pour over noodles. Bring to boiling; cover and simmer over low heat 20 minutes. Add green pepper; cover and continue cooking 10 minutes or till noodles are tender. Stir in sour cream and mushrooms; heat just through. Season to taste. Top with green-pepper rings. Makes 6 servings.

Chicken-a-la-king Casserole

1 5- or 6-ounce package
   medium noodles

. . .

1 can condensed cream of chicken soup
1 6-ounce can (⅔ cup) evaporated milk
1 teaspoon salt
1½ cups shredded process
   American cheese
2 cups diced cooked chicken or turkey
1 cup celery slices
¼ cup diced green pepper
¼ cup diced pimiento
1 cup slivered blanched almonds,
   toasted

. . .

Buttered bread crumbs

Cook noodles in boiling salted water till tender; drain. Form in nest in greased 2-quart casserole. Mix soup, milk, and salt; heat, stirring constantly. Add cheese; stir till melted. Add remaining ingredients *except* ½ cup of the almonds and the crumbs; pour over noodles. Top with crumbs and remaining almonds. Bake uncovered in hot oven (400°) about 20 minutes. Makes 6 servings.

Tomato Polenta

½ cup finely chopped onion
1 clove garlic, minced
2 tablespoons salad oil
1 1-pound can (2 cups) tomatoes
1 6-ounce can (⅔ cup) tomato paste
1 3-ounce can mushrooms and liquid
1 teaspoon salt
Dash pepper
½ teaspoon oregano

. . .

½ cup grated Parmesan cheese
1 packet or small package corn-muffin
   mix or 1 package corn-bread mix
1 8-ounce package brown-and-serve
   sausage
½ cup shredded sharp American cheese

Cook onion and garlic in hot oil till tender but not brown. Add next 6 ingredients and simmer uncovered 5 minutes.

Meanwhile add Parmesan to corn-muffin or -bread mix and prepare batter following package directions; spread in greased 10x 6x1½-inch baking dish. Slice 3 or 4 sausages over top; pour hot tomato mixture over all.

Bake in hot oven (400°) 25 minutes. Arrange remaining sausages on top; bake 15 minutes longer. Sprinkle with cheese.

Makes 5 or 6 servings.

Festive Tamale Pie

1 cup chopped onion
1 cup chopped green pepper
1 tablespoon fat
¾ pound ground beef
2 8-ounce cans (2 cups) seasoned
   tomato sauce
1 12-ounce can (1½ cups) whole kernel
   corn, drained
1 cup chopped ripe olives
1 clove garlic, minced
1 tablespoon sugar
1 teaspoon salt
2 to 3 teaspoons chili powder
Dash pepper

1½ cups shredded sharp process
   American cheese

. . .

1 recipe Corn-meal Topping

Cook onion and green pepper in hot fat till tender but not brown. Add meat; brown lightly. Add tomato sauce, corn, olives, garlic, sugar, seasonings. Simmer 20 to 25 minutes, or till thick. Add cheese; stir till melted. Pour into greased 10x6x1½-inch baking dish. Top with *Corn-meal Topping:* Stir ¾ cup yellow corn meal and ½ teaspoon salt into 2 cups cold water. Cook and stir until thick. Add 1 tablespoon butter or margarine. Mix well; spoon over meat mixture, making 3 lengthwise stripes. Bake casserole in moderate oven (375°) 40 minutes, or till top is lightly browned. Makes 6 servings.

Ham-and-Potato Scallop

5 cups thinly sliced pared potatoes
1 slice cooked (ready-to-eat type)
   smoked ham, ½ inch thick
1 can condensed cream of mushroom
   soup
¼ cup milk
½ cup chopped onion
¼ cup chopped green pepper
½ teaspoon salt
Dash pepper
Butter or margarine

Place potatoes in greased 2-quart casserole. Cut ham in serving pieces and bury in potatoes. Combine soup, milk, onion, green pepper, and seasonings; pour over potatoes. Dot with butter. Cover; bake in moderate oven (350°) 1 hour. Remove cover; bake 45 minutes longer or till potatoes are done. Before serving, fork ham to top. Trim with wreath of minced parsley. Makes 6 servings.

Supper's a flash in the pan with Skillet Spaghetti. Ground beef, and tomato join with pasta for an easy all-in-one meal that's sure to become a family favorite.

Skillet Spaghetti

In a large skillet or electric frypan, combine 1 pound ground beef, broken up; 1 cup chopped onion (2 medium onions); 2 medium cloves garlic, minced; one 8-ounce can tomato sauce; one 6-ounce can tomato paste; one 1-pint can tomato juice; 1½ cups water; 1 tablespoon chili powder; 2 teaspoons salt; dash pepper; 1 teaspoon sugar; and 1 teaspoon oregano. Cover and bring to boiling; reduce heat and simmer 30 minutes, stirring occasionally.

Add one 7- or 8-ounce package spaghetti; stir to separate strands. Simmer, covered, for 30 minutes longer or till spaghetti is tender. Stir frequently.

Add rings of onion and green pepper during the last 5 minutes of cooking, if desired. Sprinkle with grated Parmesan cheese, and serve with slices of crisp French bread, liberally buttered and oven-toasted. Pass Parmesan cheese. Makes 4 to 6 servings.

All-in-one Supper Casserole

1 10½-ounce can condensed cream of chicken soup
½ cup milk
1 cup diced cooked or canned chicken
1 cup julienne strips fully cooked or canned ham
¼ teaspoon marjoram, crushed
¼ teaspoon rosemary, crushed
1 cup drained canned peas *or* ½ 10-ounce package frozen green peas, thawed enough to break apart (about 1 cup)

. . .

1 8-ounce package frozen French-fried potato puffs

Combine soup, milk, diced chicken, ham, marjoram, rosemary, and peas; turn into 1½-quart casserole. Top with potato puffs. Bake in hot oven (425°) for 40 to 45 minutes. Makes 4 or 5 servings.

Country Casserole—tempting team-up of ham and eggs. Handy cream soup from a can lets you skip making the sauce.

Country Casserole

2 to 3 cups diced cooked or canned ham
6 hard-cooked eggs, sliced
1 6-ounce can (1⅓ cups) mushroom crowns, drained

. . .

1 can condensed cream of celery soup
½ cup milk
2 cups grated sharp process American cheese
2 teaspoons Worcestershire sauce
5 to 6 drops Tabasco

. . .

¾ cup dry medium bread crumbs
3 tablespoons melted butter or margarine

In 2-quart casserole, alternate layers of ham, egg, and mushrooms, starting and ending with ham. Combine soup and milk; add cheese, Worcestershire, and Tabasco. Heat, stirring till cheese is melted; pour over layers in casserole. Mix crumbs and butter; sprinkle over top. Bake uncovered in moderate oven (375°) about 25 minutes, or till heated through and crumbs are golden. If desired, trim with additional egg slices and sprigs of parsley. Makes 6 servings.

Chuck-wagon Beans

See them on page 6—

3 1-pound cans (6 cups) baked beans in pork and molasses sauce
1 8-ounce can seasoned tomato sauce
1 cup chopped onion
½ cup catsup
¼ cup brown sugar
2 tablespoons prepared mustard
1 teaspoon salt
4 drops Tabasco sauce
6 slices Canadian-style bacon

In 2-quart casserole or bean pot, combine beans, tomato sauce, onion, catsup, brown sugar, and seasonings. Bury bacon in beans. Bake uncovered in slow oven (300°) 3½ to 4 hours. Toward end of cooking time, fork bacon to top. Center with drained cooked or canned onions. Makes 6 servings.

Beef-hash Bake

1½ cups coarsely ground cooked beef
1 cup coarsely ground cooked potatoes
½ cup coarsely ground onion
¼ cup chopped parsley
1 teaspoon salt
Dash pepper
2 teaspoons Worcestershire sauce
1 6-ounce can (⅔ cup) evaporated milk

. . .

⅓ cup slightly crushed corn flakes
1 tablespoon butter or margarine, melted

Lightly mix beef, potatoes, onion, parsley, salt, pepper, Worcestershire, and milk. Turn into greased 1-quart casserole. Mix corn flakes and butter; sprinkle over top. Bake in moderate oven (350°) about 30 minutes. Pass catsup and mustard. Makes 4 servings.

Creamed Ham in Popovers

¼ cup butter or margarine
¼ cup enriched flour
2 cups milk
2 cups diced cooked ham
1 3-ounce can (⅔ cup) broiled sliced
   mushrooms, drained
2 tablespoons chopped green pepper
2 tablespoons pickle relish

Melt butter, blend in flour. Stir in milk gradually. Cook and stir till thick. Add next 4 ingredients; heat thoroughly. Garnish with diced pimiento. Serve in popovers, patty shells, or over hot toast points. Makes 4 or 5 servings.

Company Ham in Sour Cream

Cook 1 cup julienne strips cooked ham, and ¼ cup chopped onion in 2 tablespoons butter or margarine till onion is tender. Sprinkle with 2 teaspoons enriched flour; gradually stir in 1 cup dairy sour cream. Add one 6-ounce can (1⅓ cups) broiled sliced mushrooms, drained. Cook and stir over low heat just till mixture thickens, 2 to 3 minutes. Spoon over hot rice. Serves 3 or 4.

Jiffy Shrimp Skillet

1 can frozen condensed cream of
   shrimp soup
   •   •   •
¾ cup boiling water
⅔ cup packaged precooked rice
1 7- or 8-ounce package raw cleaned
   shrimp (about 1 pound in shell)
½ cup diced celery
½ cup diced green pepper
½ teaspoon salt
Dash pepper
   •   •   •
½ cup sliced pitted ripe olives
2 tablespoons grated Parmesan cheese*

Place soup in skillet; pour boiling water over. Cover; bring just to boiling. Stir in rice, peeled shrimp, celery, green pepper, salt, and pepper. Cover and bring to boiling; reduce heat and simmer 10 minutes or till rice and shrimp are done, stirring occasionally. Just before serving, add olives. Sprinkle with Parmesan cheese. Makes 4 servings.

*Or add 1 to 1½ teaspoons curry along with the salt and pepper, omitting Parmesan and sprinkling with ¼ cup slivered blanched almonds, toasted.

Creamed Ham in Popovers—a ladies' luncheon special! Ladle the flavorful creamed ham into puffy popovers made from a packaged mix—or spoon into patty shells or over toast points.

Club Chicken—an easy casserole

This fluffy chicken bake is loaded with good eating—just the ticket for carefree entertaining! Pass bowl of whole cranberry sauce.

Club Chicken

¼ cup butter, margarine, or chicken fat
¼ cup enriched flour
1 cup chicken broth or 1½ chicken
    bouillon cubes in 1 cup hot water
1 14½-ounce can evaporated milk
1½ teaspoons salt
2½ cups diced cooked chicken
3 cups cooked rice
1 3-ounce can (⅔ cup) broiled sliced
    mushrooms, drained
¼ cup chopped pimiento
¼ cup chopped green pepper
½ cup slivered blanched almonds,
    toasted

Melt butter; blend in flour. Gradually add broth, milk, and ½ cup water; cook and stir over low heat till thick. Add salt. Add chicken, rice, and vegetables. Pour into greased 11½x7½x1½-inch baking dish. Bake at 350° about 30 minutes. Sprinkle with almonds. Makes 8 to 10 servings.

Pressure-pan Chop Suey

1 pound pork, veal, or beef, cut in
    ½-inch cubes or thin slices
2 tablespoons fat
1 cup sliced celery
1 cup onion slices
1 cup water
½ teaspoon salt
Dash pepper
1 6-ounce can (1⅓ cups) broiled
    sliced mushrooms
¼ cup soy sauce
3 tablespoons cornstarch
1 No. 2 can (2½ cups) bean sprouts,
    drained
4 cups hot cooked rice

Brown meat slowly in hot fat in electric or standard pressure pan. Add celery, onions, water, salt, and pepper. Cover, cook at 10 pounds pressure for 5 minutes. (Check instruction book that comes with your pressure pan for possible variations in procedures.) Turn heat off. If using electric pressure pan, *disconnect cord*, too. Cool pan 5 minutes, then reduce pressure instantly by holding pan under running water. Remove pressure indicator, gauge, or control. Remove cover. Add mushrooms (with liquid). Combine soy sauce and cornstarch; tip pressure pan slightly and slowly stir cornstarch mixture into hot liquid. Cook, stirring constantly until thick. Stir in bean sprouts. Serve over hot rice. Makes 4 servings.

Lasagne Casserole

1 pound Italian sausage, bulk pork
    sausage, or ground beef
1 clove garlic, minced
1 tablespoon parsley flakes
1 tablespoon basil
1½ teaspoons salt
1 1-pound can (2 cups) tomatoes
2 6-ounce cans (1⅓ cups) tomato paste
10 ounces lasagne or wide noodles
3 cups cream-style cottage cheese
2 beaten eggs
1 teaspoon salt
½ teaspoon pepper
2 tablespoons parsley flakes
½ cup grated Parmesan cheese
1 Pound Mozzarella or American cheese,
    sliced *very thin*

Brown meat slowly; spoon off excess fat. Add next 6 ingredients. Simmer uncovered till sauce is thick, about 30 minutes, stirring occasionally.

Cook noodles in boiling salted water till tender; drain; rinse in cold water. Meanwhile combine cottage cheese with eggs, seasonings, and Parmesan cheese. Place *half* the cooked noodles in a 13x9x2-inch baking dish; spread *half* of the cottage-cheese mixture over; add *half* of the Mozzarella cheese and *half* the meat sauce. Repeat layers. Bake in moderate oven (375°) 30 minutes. Let stand 15 minutes; cut in squares. Makes 12 servings.

Chopstick Tuna

- 1 can condensed cream of mushroom soup
- 1 3-ounce can (2 cups) chow-mein noodles
- 1 6½-, 7-, or 9¼-ounce can tuna
- 1 cup sliced celery
- ½ cup salted toasted cashews
- ¼ cup chopped onion

Combine soup and ¼ cup water. Add 1 cup chow-mein noodles, the tuna, celery, cashews, onion; toss lightly. Place in ungreased 10x6x1½-inch baking dish. Sprinkle remaining noodles over top. Bake at 375° for 15 minutes or till heated through. Garnish with mandarin-orange sections. Serves 4 or 5.

To double recipe, bake in 11½x7½x1½-inch baking dish 25 minutes or till hot.

Speedy Chicken Pie

Place two 1-pound cans (4 cups) chicken fricassee in wide 3-quart saucepan (to make room for dumplings). Heat till bubbling. Add ⅓ cup milk to 1 cup packaged biscuit mix and prepare and cook dumplings according to package directions. Before serving, sprinkle with paprika. Makes 6 servings.

Chow Mein

- ½ pound pork, diced
- ¾ pound veal, diced
- ½ pound beef, diced
- 2 tablespoons fat
- ⅓ cup soy sauce
- 1 cup water
- 1 large bunch celery, in ½-inch slices
- 1 small onion, chopped
- 2 tablespoons cornstarch
- ¼ cup water
- 2 5- or 6-ounce cans water chestnuts, drained and sliced
- 1 No. 2 can (2½ cups) bean sprouts, drained
- 1 3-ounce can broiled sliced mushrooms
- Salt and pepper

Brown meats in hot fat; add soy sauce and 1 cup water; simmer 2 minutes. Add celery and onion; simmer 1½ hours.

Blend cornstarch and water; stir into meat mixture. Add chestnuts, bean sprouts, and mushrooms; heat through. Season. Serve over rice or chow-mein noodles. Makes 8 servings.

Chicken Chow Mein: Omit beef and add 2 cups diced, cooked chicken; don't brown with other meats.

Chopstick Tuna— Hostess in a hurry? Call on this canned-food wonder—quick, tasty, different. Top with mandarin-orange sections. Pass flaked coconut.

Tuna-Spaghetti Bake

½ 7-ounce package (1 cup) cut
 spaghetti, cooked and drained
1 6½-, 7-, or 9¼-ounce can tuna, flaked
⅓ cup chopped pimiento
½ cup slivered blanched almonds
1 can condensed cream of mushroom
 soup
¾ cup milk
1½ cups (6 ounces) shredded sharp
 process American cheese
½ cup crushed potato chips

In 1½-quart casserole, mix spaghetti, tuna, and pimiento. Brown almonds in 1 table-spoon butter; add soup, milk, and cheese; heat and stir till cheese melts. Pour over spaghetti. Sprinkle with chips. Bake at 350° about 30 minutes. Makes 4 or 5 servings.

Chinese Chicken Almond

½ cup sliced onion
2 tablespoons butter or margarine
1 1-pound can bean sprouts
1 8-ounce can water chestnuts, drained
1 cup celery slices
1 cup diced cooked chicken
½ cup chicken broth
1 3-ounce can broiled sliced mushrooms
3 tablespoons cornstarch
¼ teaspoon salt
¼ teaspoon monosodium glutamate
¼ cup water
2 tablespoons soy sauce
4 cups hot cooked rice

Cook onion in butter till tender, but not brown. Add bean sprouts and liquid, sliced water chestnuts, celery, chicken, broth, and mushrooms and liquid. Heat to boiling. Mix next 5 ingredients and add. Bring to boiling, stirring constantly. Serve over rice; sprinkle with ½ cup slivered blanched al-monds, toasted. Serves 4 to 6.

Chicken Italiano

2½- to 3-pound ready-to-cook frying
 chicken, cut up
1 1½-ounce envelope spaghetti-sauce
 mix
1 8-ounce can seasoned tomato sauce
1 cup water

Sprinkle chicken with salt. Brown *slowly* in small amount hot salad oil; spoon off excess fat. Combine remaining ingredients; pour over chicken. Cover; simmer 20 to 30 min-utes, or till done. Makes 4 servings.

Parsley Steak Rolls

2 pounds ¼-inch lean round steak,
 cut in 6 pieces
½ pound mushrooms
1 cup chopped parsley
¾ cup chopped onion
1 cup grated Parmesan cheese
Salt and pepper
2 tablespoons fat
1 can condensed beef consomme
• • •
2 tablespoons cornstarch
½ cup water

If meat is too thick, pound to ¼ inch. Re-serve mushroom crowns; chop stems and sprinkle over meat along with parsley, onion, and cheese; season lightly with salt, pepper. Tightly roll each piece of meat; fasten with toothpicks; lace with string. Brown slowly in hot fat. Add mushroom crowns, and consomme.

Cover; bake in moderate oven (350°) 1 hour and 15 minutes, or till tender. Remove meat rolls. Combine cornstarch and water; add to gravy; cook and stir till thick. Clip string; remove from rolls. Makes 6 servings.

Pepper Steak

1 pound ¼-inch sirloin tips, cut in
 serving pieces
2 tablespoons fat
¼ cup chopped onion
1 clove garlic, halved
1 teaspoon salt
Dash pepper
1 beef bouillon cube
1 cup hot water
• • •
1 1-pound can (2 cups) tomatoes
1 large green pepper, thinly sliced
 in rings
2 tablespoons cornstarch
¼ cup cold water
2 tablespoons soy sauce
Hot noodles

Brown meat slowly in hot fat (about 15 min-utes); add onion and garlic last few minutes. Season with salt, pepper. Dissolve bouillon cube in hot water; add to meat. Cover; sim-mer till almost tender, 20 to 25 minutes.

Add tomatoes and green pepper; cook 10 minutes longer. Combine cornstarch, cold water, soy sauce; stir into meat mixture. Bring to boiling; cook and stir 5 minutes longer. Remove garlic. Serve with hot noodles. Makes 4 servings.

Curry of Shrimp with rice—

a natural for your chafing dish

Curry of Shrimp

⅓ cup butter or margarine
½ cup chopped onion
¼ to ½ cup chopped green pepper
2 cloves garlic, minced
2 cups dairy sour cream
2 teaspoons lemon juice
2 teaspoons curry powder
¾ teaspoon salt
½ teaspoon ginger
Dash chili powder
Dash pepper
3 cups cleaned cooked or canned shrimp,
　split lengthwise in half
　(about 2 pounds in shell)

Melt butter in chafing dish or skillet. Add onion, green pepper, garlic; cook till tender. Stir in sour cream, lemon juice, and seasonings; add shrimp. Cook over *low* heat, stirring constantly just till heated through. (Sauce is traditionally thin so it can be absorbed by rice at serving time.)

To serve, spoon over hot rice or Yellow Rice. Offer curry condiments: flaked coconut, salted peanut halves, chutney, chopped hard-cooked egg. Makes 6 servings.

Yellow Rice: To 2 cups boiling water, add 1 teaspoon salt and 15 grains saffron. Stir in 1 cup uncooked long-grain rice. Return to boiling, lower heat, cover, and cook till tender, about 25 minutes. Makes 3 cups.

Lobster Newburg

⅓ cup butter or margarine
2 tablespoons enriched flour
2 cups light cream
4 beaten egg yolks
2 5-ounce cans (2 cups) lobster, cubed
½ teaspoon salt
¼ cup cooking sherry
2 teaspoons lemon juice
5 or 6 Pastry Cups

Melt butter in chafing dish or skillet; blend in flour; gradually stir in cream. Cook slowly, stirring constantly, till thick.

Stir small amount sauce into egg yolks; return to chafing dish and cook till blended, stirring constantly, about 1 minute. Add lobster and salt; heat thoroughly. Add cooking sherry and lemon juice. Serve in Pastry Cups. Sprinkle Newburg with paprika. Makes 5 or 6 servings.

Pastry Cups: Prepare packaged pastry mix according to package directions; roll ⅛ inch thick; cut in rounds with 2¼-inch cutter. Fit 5 rounds into each muffin cup (2¾ inches across top, 1½ inches deep), pressing where rounds overlap. (Press a little scrap of dough in bottom if needed.) Prick. Bake at 450° about 10 minutes. Cool.

Crab-meat Newburg: Substitute 2 cups flaked crab meat for lobster in Lobster Newburg.

Meat makes a luscious salad

Tuna-Bean Salad

1 cup dry navy beans
1 teaspoon salt
¼ cup olive oil
¼ cup white wine vinegar
½ teaspoon dry English mustard
½ teaspoon salt
1 6½-, 7-, or 9¼-ounce can tuna,
    drained and chilled
1 small red onion, thinly sliced
    and separated in rings
1 tablespoon snipped parsley

Rinse beans; add to 3 cups cold water and soak overnight. Add 1 teaspoon salt to beans and soaking water. Cover and bring to a boil; reduce heat and simmer until tender, about 1 hour. Drain and chill. In jar, combine olive oil, wine vinegar, mustard, ½ teaspoon salt and dash pepper; cover and shake well. Chill; shake again before using.

Combine chilled beans, tuna, and onion rings. Drizzle dressing over; toss lightly. Sprinkle with snipped parsley. Serves 4.

Jacques' Chicken Salad

Cut 3 thin slices from 3 large cooked and chilled chicken breasts; reserve for garnish. Cube remaining chicken. Fold ½ cup mayonnaise or salad dressing into ¼ cup whipping cream, whipped. Fold in cubed chicken, 1 cup diced celery, ½ teaspoon salt, and dash pepper; chill.

To serve, spoon salad into 3 crisp lettuce cups. Top with reserved chicken slices and a dollop of mayonnaise; sprinkle with 2 teaspoons drained capers.

Toss one 10-ounce package frozen, cooked (or one 1-pound can) French style green beans, drained and chilled, with ¼ cup Italian dressing. Arrange on platter with chicken salad. Garnish with 6 tomato slices, 6 ripe olives, and 2 hard-cooked eggs, quartered. Makes 3 servings.

Serve a salad meal!

← Tuna-Bean Salad doubles as a main dish or an appetizer. Below, julienne strips of meat and vegetables, tossed with oil and vinegar make San Marino Beef Salad.

San Marino Beef Salad

4 to 5 pounds beef short ribs
⅓ cup chopped carrot
⅓ cup chopped onion
    • • •
¼ cup olive oil
¼ cup red wine vinegar
½ teaspoon dry English mustard
½ teaspoon salt
Dash cayenne
    • • •
1 medium red onion, sliced and
    separated in rings
½ sweet red pepper, cut in julienne
    strips
3 medium carrots, cut in
    julienne strips
3 branches celery, cut in
    julienne strips
2 tablespoons cut celery leaves

Cover short ribs, chopped carrot, and onion with salted water. Bring to a boil. Cover, and simmer till tender, about 1½ to 2 hours. Remove meat from liquid. Strip from bone and trim off fat.

Cut meat in julienne strips (about 3 cups); chill. In a jar, combine olive oil, wine vinegar, mustard, salt, and cayenne. Shake well; chill. Shake again before using.

To serve, combine beef strips, onion rings, and the pepper, carrot, and celery strips. Toss with dressing. Sprinkle with cut celery leaves. Makes 4 servings.

Creamy Tuna Ring

Soften ½ envelope (1½ teaspoons) unflavored gelatin in 2 tablespoons cold water; dissolve in ¼ cup boiling water. Beat 1½ cups cream-style cottage cheese slightly; stir in dissolved gelatin, ¼ cup chopped green pepper, 2 tablespoons finely chopped green onions, and ¼ teaspoon salt. Chill till partially set. Pour into a 5-cup ring mold. Chill till almost set.

Meanwhile, soften remaining ½ envelope gelatin in 2 tablespoons cold water; dissolve *over* hot water. Mix two 6½- or 7-ounce cans tuna, drained and flaked, ½ cup chopped celery, ¾ cup mayonnaise, and 2 tablespoons lemon juice; stir in gelatin. Chill till partially set. Spoon over cheese layer. Chill till firm. Unmold. Makes 6 servings.

Party Chicken Salad

3 cups coarsely diced cooked or canned chicken
2 cups diced celery
½ cup mayonnaise or salad dressing
¼ cup chopped pickle
3 tablespoons lemon juice

Lightly toss together all ingredients. Season to taste with salt and pepper. Chill. Serve atop crisp lettuce, or in Raspberry Ring. Makes 5 servings.

Raspberry Ring: Thaw and sieve two 10-ounce packages frozen raspberries. Add enough water to make 2 cups.

Combine 2 envelopes (2 tablespoons) unflavored gelatin, ¾ cup sugar, and ¼ teaspoon salt. Add 1¼ cups boiling water, stirring to dissolve. Stir in ½ cup lemon juice and sieved berries. Chill till partially set. Fold in 1½ cups small cantaloupe balls. Pour into 6-cup ring mold. Chill till firm.

Unmold on greens. Fill ring with Party Chicken Salad. Makes 6 servings.

Meat-'n-Potato Salad

1 cup mayonnaise or salad dressing
2 tablespoons vinegar
1½ teaspoons salt
Dash pepper
2 teaspoons prepared mustard

. . .

1 12-ounce can luncheon meat, chilled
4 cups diced cooked potatoes
1½ cups sliced celery
½ cup chopped green onions
¼ cup thin radish slices
2 tablespoons minced parsley

Combine mayonnaise, vinegar, salt, pepper, and mustard. Coarsely shred meat on grater. Reserve small amount shredded meat for garnish. Add rest of meat and remaining ingredients to mayonnaise; toss lightly. Chill. Trim with hard-cooked egg wedges and reserved meat. Makes 6 to 8 servings.

Party Chicken Salad—the easy answer to what to serve at your ladies' luncheon. Seasoning is just right, lemon juice and sweet pickle subtly spike cubes of chicken. Celery is the crunch. Trim top with hard-cooked egg wedges. Serve with mayonnaise or French dressing.

Chicken-Cranberry Layers

Cranberry layer:

1 envelope (1 tablespoon) unflavored gelatin
¼ cup cold water
1 1-pound can (2 cups) whole cranberry sauce
1 9-ounce can (1 cup) crushed pineapple
½ cup broken California walnuts
1 tablespoon lemon juice

Soften gelatin in cold water; dissolve over hot water. Add remaining ingredients. Pour into 10x6x1½-inch baking dish; chill firm.

Chicken layer:

1 envelope (1 tablespoon) unflavored gelatin
¼ cup cold water
1 cup mayonnaise or salad dressing
3 tablespoons lemon juice
¾ teaspoon salt
2 cups diced cooked or canned chicken
½ cup diced celery
2 tablespoons chopped parsley

Soften gelatin in cold water; dissolve over hot water. Blend in mayonnaise, lemon juice, salt, and ½ cup water. Add chicken, celery, and parsley. Pour over cranberry layer; chill till firm.

Cut in 6 to 8 squares; invert on lettuce. Top with mayonnaise and walnut halves.

Jellied Chicken-Almond

1 envelope (1 tablespoon)
  unflavored gelatin
¼ cup cold water

• • •

1 cup mayonnaise
1 cup heavy cream, whipped
½ teaspoon salt

• • •

1½ cups diced cooked or canned chicken
¾ cup chopped blanched almonds,
  toasted
¾ cup fresh or canned green
  seedless grapes, halved

Soften gelatin in cold water; dissolve over hot water. Cool slightly; combine with mayonnaise, whipped cream, and salt.

Fold in remaining ingredients. Spoon into 6 to 8 individual molds; chill till firm. Unmold on lettuce. Top with stuffed olive slices, and peaks of mayonnaise.

Fruited Chicken Salad

3 cups diced cooked or canned chicken
1 cup diced celery
1 cup orange sections
1 9-ounce can (1 cup) pineapple tidbits,
  drained
½ cup slivered almonds, toasted
2 tablespoons salad oil
2 tablespoons orange juice
2 tablespoons vinegar
½ teaspoon salt
Dash marjoram
½ cup mayonnaise or salad dressing

Combine first 5 ingredients. Blend salad oil, orange juice, vinegar, and seasonings. Add to chicken mixture. Chill 1 hour. Drain. Add mayonnaise; toss. Makes 8 to 10 servings.

Turkey-Green Grape Toss

1½ cups diced cooked turkey
1 cup thinly sliced celery
½ cup fresh or canned green seedless
  grapes
½ cup mayonnaise or salad dressing
½ teaspoon seasoned salt

Combine turkey, celery, grapes, and mayonnaise. Sprinkle with seasoned salt and dash pepper. Toss lightly. Serve on greens and trim with small bunch of grapes. Or serve in avocado halves brushed with lemon juice. Makes 6 servings.

Golden Chicken Salad

1 pound fresh asparagus or 1 10-ounce
  package frozen asparagus spears
Italian dressing

• • •

½ cup mayonnaise or salad dressing
1 teaspoon lemon juice
½ teaspoon turmeric
2 tablespoons finely chopped chives

• • •

1½ cups diced cooked or canned chicken
½ cup diced celery
2 hard-cooked eggs, diced
½ teaspoon salt

Cook asparagus; drain. Marinate in Italian dressing 2 hours in refrigerator, turning once or twice. Combine mayonnaise, lemon juice, turmeric, and chives; set aside.

Mix remaining ingredients; add mayonnaise mixture; toss lightly. Chill. Arrange drained asparagus on lettuce; top with the salad Dash with paprika. Serves 4.

Tuna-stuffed Tomatoes—party fare! Serve with hot consomme, and tiny sandwiches.

For tuna salad: Break one 6½- or 7-ounce can tuna in chunks; sprinkle with 1 tablespoon lemon juice. Add 2 hard-cooked eggs, chopped, ¼ cup thinly sliced sweet pickle, ¼ cup finely chopped onion, 2 tablespoons diced pimiento, ¼ teaspoon salt, and dash pepper. Add ⅓ cup mayonnaise; mix gently; chill.

Turn 4 tomatoes stem end down. Cut each, *not quite through*, in 6 equal sections. Salt inside; fill with tuna salad; serve on lettuce.

Sea-food salads—simple and smart

Sea-food Salad

1 5- or 6½-ounce can tuna, crab, lobster,
  or shrimp, or 1 cup any sea food
1 to 2 tablespoons lemon juice
1 cup sliced celery
¼ cup salad dressing or mayonnaise
Salt and pepper to taste

Break sea food in chunks or flake it, if necessary. Sprinkle with lemon juice. Add celery
and salad dressing. Mix lightly; season.
Chill. Serve with lemon wedges. Makes 4
servings.

Crab Salad with Cucumber: Follow directions
for Sea-food Salad, using crab. Add ¼ cup
diced unpared cucumber just before serving. Top with hard-cooked egg slices, capers.

Lobster in Avocado Shells: Follow directions
for Sea-food Salad, using lobster. Mound
salad in 4 lemon-juice-brushed avocado
halves. Trim with orange sections.

Shrimp in Lime Ring

2½ to 3 cups cooked cleaned shrimp
Clear French or Italian dressing
  • • •
1 package lime-flavored gelatin
¾ cup hot water
  • • •
¾ cup drained shredded or ground
  unpared cucumber*
¼ cup finely sliced green onions
1 cup large-curd cream-style
  cottage cheese
1 cup mayonnaise or salad dressing
1 teaspoon horseradish
¼ teaspoon salt

Chill shrimp several hours in dressing, turning them occasionally. Meanwhile dissolve
gelatin in hot water. Chill till partially set.
Combine remaining ingredients; mix well.
Stir into gelatin mixture.
  Turn into 5-cup ring mold. Chill till set.
Unmold; fill center with drained shrimp,
add ruffle of water cress. Pass bowl of mayonnaise or salad dressing. Makes 6 servings.
  *If cucumbers are mature, discard seeds
before shredding or grinding.

Crab Luncheon Salad

½ cup dairy sour cream
½ cup mayonnaise or salad dressing
1 tablespoon white wine vinegar
½ 2-ounce can anchovy fillets,
  drained and minced
3 tablespoons sliced green onion tops
3 tablespoons finely snipped parsley
Romaine, torn in pieces
2 7½-ounce cans crab meat, drained
6 hard-cooked eggs, thinly sliced
1 medium cucumber, thinly sliced
Lemon wedges

Combine sour cream, mayonnaise, vinegar,
anchovies, onion tops, and parsley for dressing. Mix well and chill. Arrange romaine on
6 chilled salad plates. Arrange crab, eggs,
and cucumber on romaine. Garnish with
lemon. Pass dressing. Makes 6 servings.

Green Goddess Salad

1 cup mayonnaise or salad dressing
2 tablespoons anchovy paste
1 teaspoon Worcestershire sauce
½ teaspoon dry mustard
1 clove garlic, minced
3 tablespoons chopped chives or
  green onions
2 tablespoons finely chopped cooked
  cleaned shrimp
1 hard-cooked egg, finely chopped
  • • •
½ head romaine
1 bunch leaf lettuce
  • • •
1 cup cooked cleaned shrimp, chilled
1 stalk French endive, sliced
3 medium tomatoes, quartered
½ cup julienne-style cooked beets,
  drained and chilled

Combine the mayonnaise, anchovy paste,
Worcestershire, mustard, and garlic. Stir in
chives, chopped shrimp, and egg. Chill.
Makes 1½ cups Green Goddess Dressing.
  At serving time, break up romaine and
leaf lettuce in bite-size pieces. Place on salad
plates. Arrange shrimp, endive, tomatoes,
and beets atop. Spoon Green Goddess
Dressing over. Serves 6 to 8.

Tuna Parfait Mold. Easy is the keynote for this make-ahead salad with built-in dressing. Delicious—shiny gelatin full of tuna, celery, and olives. Chili sauce gives a pretty pink.

Canned tuna comes several ways—solid pack with large pieces, chunk style with bite-size pieces, and grated and flaked.

Crab Louis

1 cup mayonnaise or salad
   dressing
¼ cup heavy cream, whipped
¼ cup chili sauce
¼ cup chopped green pepper
¼ cup chopped green onions
   and tops
1 teaspoon lemon juice
Salt

. . .

1 large head lettuce
2 to 3 cups cooked crab meat, or
   2 6½-ounce cans, chilled
2 large tomatoes, cut in wedges
2 hard-cooked eggs, cut in wedges
Paprika

Combine mayonnaise, whipped cream, chili sauce, green pepper, green onion, and lemon juice. Salt to taste. Chill. Makes about 2 cups of Louis Dressing.

Line 4 large plates with lettuce leaves. Shred rest of lettuce and arrange on leaves. Remove bits of shell from crab meat. Reserve claw meat; leave remainder in chunks and arrange atop lettuce. Circle with wedges of tomato and egg. Sprinkle with salt.

Pour ¼ cup Louis Dressing over each salad. Sprinkle with paprika. Top with reserved claw meat. Pass remaining dressing.

Makes 4 servings.

Tuna Parfait Mold

2 envelopes (2 tablespoons) unflavored
   gelatin
1 cup cold water
1 cup boiling water
1 cup mayonnaise
½ cup chili sauce
3 to 4 tablespoons lemon juice
¼ teaspoon salt
2 6½- or 7-ounce cans (2 cups) tuna,
   flaked
1 cup chopped celery
½ cup stuffed green olive slices

Soften gelatin in cold water; dissolve in boiling water. Cool. Combine the mayonnaise, chili sauce, lemon juice, and salt. Stir in the gelatin and mix well. Chill till partially set. Stir in tuna, celery, and olives. Pour into 1½-quart melon mold; chill till firm. Unmold on crisp lettuce. Serve with hard-cooked egg wedges. Makes 8 to 10 servings.

Salmon-salad Loaf

1 package lemon-flavored gelatin
1 cup boiling water
½ cup cold water
3 tablespoons vinegar
½ cup mayonnaise or salad dressing
¼ teaspoon salt
1 1-pound can (2 cups) salmon, drained
   and coarsely flaked
1 cup chopped celery
¼ cup chopped parsley
¼ cup chopped onion

Dissolve gelatin in boiling water. Add cold water, vinegar, mayonnaise, and salt. Beat well; chill till partially set. Beat till fluffy; fold in remaining ingredients. Pour into 8½x4½x2½-inch loaf pan. Chill till set. Unmold on crisp greens. Serves 6.

Shrimp-Avocado Bowls

½ head lettuce
½ head curly endive
1 cup cooked or canned cleaned shrimp,
   drained
3 hard-cooked eggs, sliced
1 avocado, sliced
Water cress
Clear French dressing

Tear lettuce and endive in bite-size pieces in individual salad bowls. Top with shrimp, egg slices, and avocado. Trim with water cress. Pass dressing. Makes 6 servings.

Make supper a sandwich!

Double-beef Sandwiches

There's dried beef and corned beef both in this Dutch-lunch special!—

12 slices rye bread, buttered
2 tablespoons prepared mustard
Leaf lettuce
4 ounces dried beef, pulled apart
4 ounces sliced Muenster or brick cheese
4 ounces cooked or canned corned beef, sliced very thin
2 large dill pickles, thinly sliced
1 onion, thinly sliced
1 tablespoon prepared horseradish

Spread half the bread slices with mustard and add layers of lettuce, dried beef, cheese, corned beef, pickle, and onion. Top each stack-up with more lettuce. Spread remaining bread slices with horseradish, and complete sandwiches. Anchor with toothpick topped with a ripe olive. Makes 6.

Grilled Crab Sandwiches

1 6½- or 7½-ounce can (about 1 cup) crab meat, drained and flaked
½ cup shredded sharp process American cheese
¼ cup chopped celery
2 tablespoons drained sweet-pickle relish
2 tablespoons chopped green onions and tops
1 hard-cooked egg, chopped
3 tablespoons salad dressing or mayonnaise
½ teaspoon lemon juice
½ teaspoon prepared horseradish
10 slices bread, buttered generously
5 tomato slices

Combine first 9 ingredients; spread on *un-buttered* side of 5 bread slices. Add tomato slices; season with salt and pepper. Top with bread slices, buttered side up. Grill till sandwiches are golden brown. Makes 5.

Cotto Tree

1 head leaf lettuce
1 large cucumber (about 8 inches)
1 13-ounce package (17 to 20 slices) sliced bologna
2 7-ounce packages (10 to 12 slices each) sliced Cotto salami
Olives, ripe and stuffed green

Wash lettuce; pat dry. Cut cucumber to measure about 7 inches; press cut surface on needle-point flower holder. Attach lettuce to cover cucumber, using toothpick halves to hold leaves in place. (Fold or tear larger leaves.) With sharp knife, make a cut in salami and bologna slices (or any round luncheon meat) from center to edge. Wrap cut luncheon meat around finger in a spiral fashion. Fasten with a toothpick from the inside, leaving part of the end of the toothpick extending into center of spiral. (Olive garnish will be attached to this later.) With other end of toothpick, attach spiral to cucumber "tree." Be sure lettuce peeks out from between spirals. Spear centers of spirals with olives.

Chef's Salad in a Roll

Brown big brown-and-serve French rolls (about 8 inches long) according to package directions. Split in half, but *not quite through.* For *each* sandwich, line bottom half of roll with romaine lettuce; drizzle with 1 teaspoon French dressing. Pile on slices of chicken; dash with salt and pepper. Add 1 or 2 slices boiled ham and Swiss cheese, halved to fit roll. Top with hard-cooked egg slices; salt. Cover with romaine and tomato slices; season. Drizzle with 2 teaspoons more dressing. Add roll tops, anchor with toothpicks.

Serve a luncheon centerpiece →

For your next patio party, surround a Cotto Tree with an assortment of luncheon meats and parsley- or mustard-buttered breads.

Shrimp Boat

A hint of horseradish is the secret. Serve with coffee and you have a meal—

3 cups cooked or canned cleaned
    shrimp
1 cup diced celery
4 hard-cooked eggs, chopped
⅓ cup sliced green onions
¼ cup chopped dill pickle
2 tablespoons drained capers
    (optional)
1 cup mayonnaise or salad dressing
2 tablespoons chili sauce
2 teaspoons prepared horseradish
1 teaspoon salt

. . .

1 unsliced loaf Vienna bread,
    about 11x5 inches
Melted butter or margarine

. . .

Leaf lettuce

Reserve a few large shrimp for garnish; cut up remainder. Combine shrimp, celery, eggs, onions, pickles, and capers. Blend mayonnaise and seasonings; add to shrimp mixture and toss lightly. Chill. Cut a large deep wedge out of Vienna loaf. Brush the cut surfaces with melted butter. Place loaf on ungreased baking sheet and toast in moderate oven (350°) for 15 minutes. Cool before filling.

Line bread "boat" with lettuce; mound with shrimp salad. Trim with whole shrimp and "sails" of lemon slices. Pass lemon wedges. Slice the loaf into 6 to 8 servings.

Oriental Tuna Sandwich

A special luncheon treat for the ladies (and men, too!). The filling may also be chilled and served in lettuce cups as a summer salad—

Blend ½ cup mayonnaise or salad dressing with 2 tablespoons minced onion, 2 teaspoons lemon juice, 2 teaspoons soy sauce, and 1 teaspoon curry powder. Add two 6½- or 7-ounce cans tuna, drained, and one 5-ounce can (½ cup) water chestnuts, drained and sliced; toss lightly.

Cut one loaf of French bread in half lengthwise; wrap top half and store for use later. Spread bottom half with soft butter or margarine. Top with lettuce and tuna filling. Garnish with cherry tomatoes, halved, and avocado slices. Makes 6 to 8 servings.

Hong Kong Hamburgers

1 pound ground beef
1 8½-ounce can sliced pineapple
⅓ cup brown sugar
2 teaspoons cornstarch
3 tablespoons red wine vinegar
1 tablespoon soy sauce
1 tablespoon Worcestershire sauce
4 green-pepper rings
4 hamburger buns, split and toasted

Shape meat in 4 patties; sprinkle with salt and pepper. Broil 4 inches from heat 10 minutes; turn once. Meanwhile drain pineapple, reserving ¼ cup syrup. Mix sugar and cornstarch; blend in pineapple syrup, wine vinegar, soy sauce, and Worcestershire sauce. Cook and stir in small skillet till mixture boils. Add pineapple slices; top with pepper rings. Cover; heat through.

Place burgers on buns; top with pineapple and pepper slices. Spoon a little of the sauce over each burger; pass extra sauce.

Pizza by the Yard

A fast way to have pizza—French bread is the easy crust—

1 loaf French bread, about
    18 inches long
1 pound ground beef
⅓ cup grated Parmesan cheese
¼ cup finely chopped onion
¼ cup chopped pitted ripe olives
1 teaspoon salt
½ to 1 teaspoon crushed oregano
Dash pepper
1 6-ounce can (⅔ cup) tomato
    paste

. . .

3 tomatoes, peeled and sliced
6 slices sharp process American
    or Mozzarella cheese, halved
    diagonally

Cut French loaf lengthwise in half. Combine ground meat with Parmesan cheese, chopped onion, olives, salt, oregano, pepper, and tomato paste. Spread evenly on each half loaf. Broil about 5 inches from heat 12 minutes or till meat is done.

Alternate tomato and cheese slices on tops of loaves. Broil 1 to 2 minutes more or just till cheese slices begin to melt. Cut each half loaf in 4 or 5 slices. For pizza lovers, count on 2 slices apiece. Makes 4 to 5 servings.

Burgundy Beefburgers

Burger sophisticate, deliciously flavored with butter and wine—

2 pounds ground chuck*
1 cup soft bread crumbs
1 egg
¼ cup red cooking wine (not sweet)
2 tablespoons sliced green onions
1 teaspoon salt
Dash pepper
. . .
2 tablespoons sliced green
onions and tops
½ cup butter or margarine
¼ cup red cooking wine
Butter or margarine
6 thick slices French bread, cut
diagonally

In a large bowl, toss ground chuck, bread crumbs, egg, cooking wine, onions, salt, and pepper together with a fork till well mixed. Shape in 6 doughnut-shaped burgers, about 1 inch thick. For burgundy sauce, cook 2 tablespoons green onions in ½ cup butter till just tender; add ¼ cup wine. Brush burgers with the sauce. Broil about 4 inches from heat for 9 minutes, brushing frequently with sauce. Turn burgers and broil 4 minutes longer or till of desired doneness, continuing to brush with sauce.

Serve on buttered French bread slices. Heat remaining wine sauce to pass with burgers. Makes 6 servings.

*If beef is lean, have 4 ounces suet ground with this amount of meat.

Dad's Denvers

A short cut to the popular Denver sandwich— packaged omelet mix studded with bits of ham, onion, and green pepper—

Cut one loaf of French bread in half lengthwise; wrap top half and store for use later. Toast bottom half; spread with one 4½-ounce can (⅔ cup) deviled ham. Prepare one 1 5/6-ounce package western omelet mix according to package directions; scramble mixture instead of making omelet.

Pile eggs over deviled ham. Top with 4 tomato slices; place one half slice of sharp process American cheese over each tomato slice. Place loaf on baking sheet; broil about 4 inches from heat just till cheese melts. Makes 4 servings.

Pizza Pronto

A sure treat when the younger clan has a get-together. So easy to fix, everyone can relax—

With palms of hands, flatten two 8-ounce packages refrigerated biscuits to 4½x2-inch ovals. On greased baking sheet, arrange 10 biscuits at slight angles to each other, in two adjoining rows. Press adjoining ends together securely. On another baking sheet, repeat with remaining 10 biscuits.

Combine one 8-ounce can (1 cup) tomato sauce, 1 teaspoon instant minced onion, ¼ teaspoon oregano, and ¼ teaspoon garlic salt; spread evenly over the two pizzas to within ½ inch of edges. Sprinkle pizzas with one 4-ounce package (1 cup) shredded sharp Cheddar cheese; top with 2 slices (3 ounces) Mozzerella cheese torn in small pieces. Arrange one 6-ounce can (about 1 cup) broiled mushroom crowns, drained, over pizzas.

Bake in a hot oven (450°) for 8 to 10 minutes, or till edges of pizza crusts are golden brown. If desired, garnish with ½ cup pitted ripe olives, halved lengthwise. Makes 2 pizzas, 4 to 5 servings each.

Hot Avocado-Crab Sandwich

Hot toasted English muffins make the base—

1 10½-ounce can condensed cream of
mushroom soup
¼ cup milk
½ teaspoon Worcestershire sauce
Dash bottled hot pepper sauce
. . .
1 cup shredded sharp process
American cheese
4 large English muffins, split,
toasted, and buttered
1 7½-ounce can (1 cup) crab meat,
flaked
2 avocadoes, peeled and sliced
½ cup shredded sharp process
American cheese

Combine mushroom soup, milk, Worcestershire sauce, and pepper sauce; heat, stirring occasionally. Add 1 cup cheese; stir till melted. Place muffins on baking sheet. Spread rounded tablespoon sauce on each muffin; top with crab meat, then avocado slices. Drizzle with remaining sauce. Sprinkle with ½ cup cheese.

Broil about 4 inches from heat 3 to 4 minutes or till sandwiches are golden brown and bubbly. Makes 8 sandwiches.

Champion Roast Beef Sandwiches

Roast beef on dark rye with the extra zip of horseradish and onion—that's a winning combination in anyone's book—

8 slices dark rye bread
Butter or margarine
½ cup dairy sour cream
2 teaspoons dry onion-soup mix
2 teaspoons prepared horseradish, well drained
Dash freshly ground pepper

. . .

Thinly sliced cold roast beef
Leaf lettuce, chilled

Spread bread slices with butter. Combine sour cream, onion-soup mix, horseradish, and pepper. Spread about 1 tablespoon of the sour-cream mixture on each slice of bread. Top 4 slices with roast beef, then lettuce; cover with remaining bread. Makes 4.

Square Burgers

1 teaspoon instant minced onion
½ cup evaporated milk
1½ pounds ground chuck
1 slightly beaten egg
1 teaspoon salt
¼ teaspoon monosodium glutamate
Dash pepper
4 slices white bread, toasted and buttered
1 3½-ounce can onion rings *or*
1 4-ounce package frozen

Soak onion in evaporated milk for 5 minutes; lightly mix with meat, egg, and seasonings. Place meat mixture on large sheet of waxed paper; lightly pat into a 9-inch square. Cut meat in 4 squares. With scissors, cut through waxed paper between burgers. Place, meat side down, on broiler rack; peel off waxed paper. Broil 4 to 5 inches from heat for 5 minutes; turn and broil 3 to 4 minutes longer or till of desired doneness.

Meanwhile, heat onion rings according to the label directions. Place each burger on a slice of toast; top with onion rings. Pass catsup and mustard. Makes 4 servings.

Skewer Dogs

There's a frankfurter surprise in the center of each ground-beef kabob—

1 pound ground beef
¾ cup soft bread crumbs
¼ cup milk
2 tablespoons chopped onion
1 slightly beaten egg
½ teaspoon salt
Dash pepper
6 frankfurters
1 cup catsup
¼ cup butter or margarine, melted
¼ cup molasses
2 tablespoons vinegar
6 slices bacon (optional)

Combine first 7 ingredients; mix lightly. Divide meat mixture into 6 portions. Shape meat around franks, covering completely. (Roll kabobs between waxed paper to make uniform.) Chill. Insert skewers lengthwise through frankfurters. For Sauce: Combine catsup, butter, molasses, and vinegar; brush over kabobs. Wrap each kabob spiral-fashion with slice of bacon; secure with toothpicks. Broil 3 inches from heat about 15 minutes, turning as needed to cook bacon. Simmer sauce while kabobs are cooking; brush on kabobs just before removing from heat. Serve in toasted coney buns; pass extra sauce. Makes 6 sandwiches.

Hot Ham Buns

Poppy seeds add a touch of old-world flavor here. Try rye hamburger buns for a change—

¼ cup soft butter or margarine
2 tablespoons prepared horseradish-mustard
2 teaspoons poppy seed
2 tablespoons finely chopped onion
4 hamburger buns, split
4 thin slices boiled ham
4 slices process Swiss cheese

Mix butter, mustard, poppy seed, and onion; spread on cut surfaces of buns. Tuck a slice of ham and cheese in each bun. Arrange on baking sheet. Bake sandwiches in moderate oven (350°) for about 20 minutes or till hot through. Makes 4 sandwiches.

Shrimp Luncheon Sandwiches

With a beautifully arranged fruit plate, these make a great bridge snack—

1 3-ounce package cream cheese, softened
2 tablespoons mayonnaise or salad dressing
1 tablespoon catsup
1 teaspoon prepared mustard
Dash garlic powder

• • •

1 cup chopped canned or cooked cleaned shrimp
¼ cup finely chopped celery
1 teaspoon finely chopped onion

• • •

10 slices lightly buttered sandwich bread

Blend softened cheese with mayonnaise; mix in catsup, mustard, and garlic powder. Stir in shrimp, celery, and onion. Use as a filling between slices of lightly buttered sandwich bread. Trim crusts, if desired. Cut each sandwich diagonally in 4 triangles. Makes 1 cup filling—enough for 20 tea sandwiches.

Circle 'Round Sandwich

Petite cherry tomatoes go with this whopper. To save time make the filling ahead—

Combine 6 hard-cooked eggs, chopped, ¼ cup chopped onion, 2 tablespoons chopped canned pimiento, 2 tablespoons chopped green olives, and one 12-ounce can luncheon meat, finely diced (about 2 cups). Blend ½ cup mayonnaise or salad dressing, ¼ teaspoon salt, and dash pepper. Add to first mixture and toss lightly; chill.

Cut two 1-inch-thick slices from the bottom of 1 large round loaf of unsliced bread. Using a biscuit cutter, remove center section of *each* slice (should leave about a 2-inch rim). Spread meat and egg salad filling over bottom slice. Spread second slice with softened butter or margarine; top with 6 large lettuce leaves. Place over salad mixture. Cut sandwich ring in 10 individual sandwiches.

If desired, top with *Bologna-cheese wedges:* Make 2 stack-ups of bologna and cheese slices, alternating 5 slices of bologna with 4 slices of cheese for each stack-up. Trim cheese corners; cut each stack in 5 wedges.

Sandwiches go big!

Circle 'Round Sandwich cuts in generous help-yourself servings. Large round bread slices sandwich a delicious filling of diced luncheon meat and hard-cooked egg. Bologna-cheese wedges top all.

Piquant sauces–lively accents for

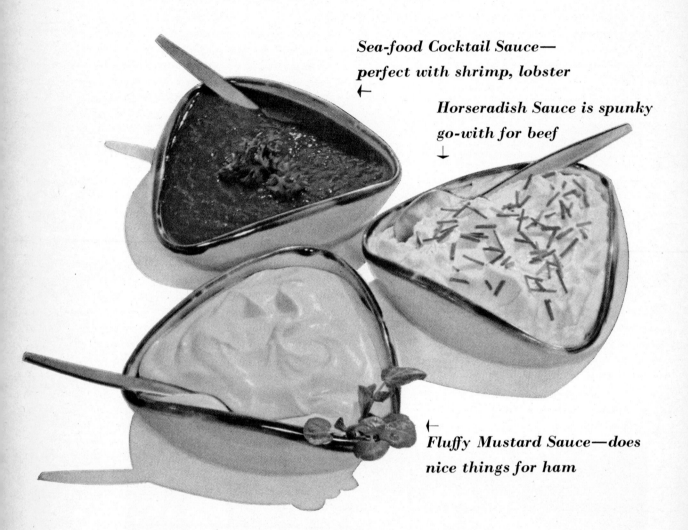

Sea-food Cocktail Sauce—
perfect with shrimp, lobster
←

Horseradish Sauce is spunky
go-with for beef
↓

←
Fluffy Mustard Sauce—does
nice things for ham

Sea-food Cocktail Sauce

Appetizer favorite: Chilled shrimp dunked
in this tangy sauce—

⅓ cup chili sauce
2 tablespoons lemon juice
1½ tablespoons horseradish
¼ teaspoon grated onion
1 teaspoon Worcestershire sauce
2 drops Tabasco sauce
Salt to taste

Combine ingredients and chill thoroughly.
Serve with sea food. Makes about ½ cup.

Warren's Barbecue Sauce

1 cup catsup
1 tablespoon Worcestershire sauce
Few drops Tabasco sauce
1 cup water
¼ cup vinegar
1 tablespoon sugar
1 teaspoon salt
1 teaspoon celery seed

Combine all ingredients. Heat to boiling.
Let simmer 30 minutes. Makes enough sauce
for basting 4 pounds spareribs.
(More barbecue sauces, pages 156, 157.)

meat and fish

Fluffy Mustard Sauce

2 beaten egg yolks
1 tablespoon sugar
3 tablespoons prepared mustard
2 tablespoons vinegar
1 tablespoon water
¾ teaspoon salt
1 tablespoon butter or margarine
1 tablespoon prepared horseradish
½ cup heavy cream, whipped

To egg yolks, add sugar, mustard, vinegar, water, and salt; mix well. Cook over *hot, not boiling*, water, stirring constantly, till thick, about 4 or 5 minutes. Blend in butter and horseradish. Cool thoroughly.

Fold in whipped cream. Makes 1½ cups. Store in refrigerator. To serve with warm meat, remove from refrigerator 30 minutes before mealtime. Delicious with ham or ham loaf.

Note: See hot Mustard Sauce on page 69.

Trader Vic's Chinese Mustard

¼ cup boiling water
¼ cup dry English mustard
½ teaspoon salt
2 teaspoons salad oil
Turmeric (optional)

Stir boiling water into dry mustard. Add salt and salad oil. If sauce is not yellow enough, add some turmeric. Serve with pork or French-fried Shrimp. Makes ⅓ cup.

Jiffy Mustard Sauce

Mix 1 cup dairy sour cream, 2 tablespoons prepared mustard, and 1 teaspoon prepared horseradish. Chill. Serve with pork chops.

Horseradish Sauce

1 8-ounce package cream cheese, softened
2 to 3 tablespoons horseradish

With electric mixer, beat cream cheese till fluffy. Beat in horseradish. Makes 1½ cups. Chill if made early. Top with minced chives.

Raisin Sauce for Ham

½ cup brown sugar
1 teaspoon dry mustard
2 tablespoons cornstarch

• • •

1 tablespoon vinegar
2 tablespoons lemon juice
¼ teaspoon grated lemon peel
1½ cups water
½ cup raisins

Mix brown sugar, dry mustard, and cornstarch. Slowly add vinegar. Add lemon juice and peel, water, and raisins. Stir over low heat till thick. Makes 2 cups. Serve hot with ham.

Cherry Sauce

Combine 1 tablespoon cornstarch, ½ cup sugar, and one 1-pound can (2 cups) pitted tart red cherries. Cook, stirring constantly, over low heat till thick and clear. Add a few drops red food coloring if desired. Serve hot with sliced ham or tongue.

Makes about 2 cups sauce.

Quick Cranberry Sauce

2 cups sugar
2 cups water

• • •

1 pound (4 cups) cranberries

Combine sugar and water in saucepan; stir to dissolve sugar. Heat to boiling and boil 5 minutes. Add cranberries and cook till skins pop, about 5 minutes. Remove from heat. Serve warm or chilled.

Makes about 4 cups.

Mint Sauce

Add ⅓ cup chopped mint leaves and 2 tablespoons sugar to ½ cup hot vinegar; stir till sugar dissolves. Serve with lamb.

In-a-hurry Mint Sauce: Heat ½ cup mint jelly slowly, stirring occasionally, till melted. Serve with lamb.

Lemon-Butter Sauce

Combine ½ cup butter or margarine, melted, 2 tablespoons lemon juice, and 1 tablespoon chopped parsley. Makes a good basting sauce or go-with for fish and sea food.

Note: Tartare Sauce on page 101.

Main dishes to freeze, heat, and eat

You'll be meals ahead with main dishes in the freezer. Use frozen cooked foods within 1 or 2 months

Barbecued Spareribs

Come and get 'em a few months later! Cool barbecued ribs (recipe, page 39) quickly and thoroughly. Wrap enough for one meal in heavy foil. Seal by folding edges over several times and pressing tightly. Freeze at once. *To serve*, reheat frozen ribs, foil wrapped, or in covered pan, in hot oven (400°) 30 to 40 minutes.

Meat Balls and Spaghetti

Freeze this specialty (recipe, page 75) in an oven-going 2-quart casserole that travels from freezer right to the oven. *To serve*, reheat frozen casserole, uncovered, in moderate oven (350°) about 1½ hours. Serve over freshly cooked spaghetti (one 8-ounce package). Pass bowl of grated Parmesan cheese.

Shrimp Curry

2 tablespoons butter or margarine
1½ cups finely chopped pared tart
   apples

• • •

2 tablespoons enriched flour
2 teaspoons curry powder
1 teaspoon salt
2 cups milk
2 cups cleaned cooked shrimp

Melt butter; add apples and cook 5 minutes. Combine flour, curry powder, and salt; stir into apples. Add milk slowly; cook and stir till thick. Add shrimp. Cool quickly to room temperature. Pack in freezing containers. Seal and freeze immediately.

To serve: Remove from freezer containers and place in 1½-quart saucepan or top of double boiler. Reheat over low heat or over boiling water till thawed and heated through. Stir occasionally. Serve with 3 cups hot, fluffy rice; dash shrimp sauce with paprika. Makes 5 to 7 servings.

Meat loaf on the double

Fix meat loaves in pairs—save mixing and measuring another day.

Bake loaves in foilware tray; cool. Wrap tray and all in saran wrapping or foil. Seal loose ends; freeze.

To serve, unwrap loaf; heat at 350° about 1½ hours or till hot through.

Or bake individual loaves; freeze. Heating time can be cut in half.

So handy—cooked chicken

Stew each chicken for freezing in separate kettle (recipe, page 98).

Cool quickly. Remove chicken from bones. Pack white, dark meat separately in freezer containers or wrap tightly in foil. Freeze. *To serve:* For salads, thaw wrapped in refrigerator; for hot dishes, thaw in covered pan in moderate oven (350°).

Freeze favorite meat stew

Make lamb, beef, or veal stew. (See index for recipes.) Be careful not to overcook. Cool stew quickly by placing uncovered cooking pan in sink of cold water that's chilled with plenty of ice cubes. When the stew's cold, pour into the freezer containers. Seal tightly, label, and freeze at once.

To serve, heat stew over low heat.

Cheese-Meat Loaf

   1½ pounds ground beef
   1½ cups dry bread crumbs
   ⅔ cup diced process American cheese
   ½ cup chopped onion
   2 tablespoons chopped green pepper
   2 teaspoons salt
   1 small bay leaf, crushed
   Dash thyme
   Dash garlic salt

        • • •

   2 beaten eggs
   1 8-ounce can (1 cup) seasoned tomato sauce

Combine beef, crumbs, cheese, onion, green pepper, and seasonings; mix thoroughly. Add eggs to tomato sauce; blend into meat mixture. Form in 2 loaves in 9½x6½x1½-inch foilware tray or shallow baking pan. Bake in moderate oven (350°) about 1 hour. Cool thoroughly; wrap; freeze.

To serve: Heat, unwrapped, in moderate oven (350°) about 1½ hours or till heated through. Makes 8 to 10 servings.

Freeze Hamburger Bake for no-fuss dinner

Follow directions for Hamburger Bake, page 142. Quickly pack the cooled meat mixture in foilware pan; do not add topper. Label, adjust cover, freeze. *To serve*, heat uncovered at 350° about 1½ hours. Increase temperature to 425°; top with Lattice Cheese Crust. Bake about 15 minutes longer.

Hot sandwiches for lunch in jig time! →

Smart cook! Freezer holds supply of meat sandwiches —ham, meat loaf, or roast beef. Slice meat thin for quick thawing; put a generous number of layers in each sandwich. *To serve*, dip frozen sandwiches in egg-and-milk mixture as for French toast, and grill about 4 minutes on each side. Serve piping hot.

← Cool to-be-frozen foods at once

Best way is to immediately set pan of cooked food (here it's Shrimp Curry; could be Chicken a la King) in bowl, pan, or sink containing cold water with ice. When cooled to room temperature, ladle into freezer containers. Write name of dish and date on lids with grease pencil. Adjust covers and freeze.

Hamburger Bake

1⅔ cups minced onion
1¼ cups chopped celery
½ cup minced green pepper
3 tablespoons butter or margarine
2 pounds ground beef
2 cans condensed tomato soup
1 to 2 teaspoons chili powder
1½ teaspoons salt
¼ teaspoon pepper
2 cloves garlic, minced

• • •

Lattice Cheese Crust

Cook onion, celery, and green pepper in butter till tender but not brown, about 5 minutes. Add ground beef and cook till lightly browned. Add remaining ingredients; mix well. Cool quickly to room temperature. Put in 9x1½-inch round foilware pan. Cover and freeze. Makes 6 servings.

To serve: Leave frozen mixture in pan. Place, uncovered, in moderate oven (350°) till heated through, about 1½ hours. Increase temperature to 425°; top with Lattice Cheese Crust, and bake about 15 minutes longer or till done.

Lattice Cheese Crust: Sift together 1 cup sifted enriched flour, 1 teaspoon baking powder, and ½ teaspoon salt. Cut in 2 tablespoons shortening; stir in ¼ cup shredded sharp process American cheese. Add ⅓ cup milk and mix just till moistened. Turn out on lightly floured surface; roll ⅜ inch thick; cut in ⅜-inch strips. Weave.

Gravy—for the freezer

Reheat leftover gravy before freezing; chill. Package and freeze. Handy tip: Freeze small amounts in clean juice-concentrate or tomato-sauce cans. Unmold, seal in pint polyethylene bags. Label so you'll know which kind's which. Put several bags in a big one to save hunting.

Meat canning

Meats may be packed precooked or raw for canning. Pack meat loosely in jars to no more than 1 inch of jar top. Add 1 teaspoon salt per quart for raw or precooked meat. To precooked meats, add 3 or 4 tablespoons liquid; water or meat stock may be used. Never add liquid to meats packed raw. Wipe all grease or meat particles from top of jar. Adjust cap according to the directions.

A pressure cooker is recommended for processing meats. Process 1 hour and 15 minutes at 10 pounds pressure, following manufacturer's directions. Canned meats must be boiled in an open pan 10 to 15 minutes before using.

Meat freezing guide

Freezing meats, poultry, fish

Packaging and wrapping. Keep packages small for rapid freezing and make them family-size units—1 roast, 3 or 4 chops, 6 to 8 ground-meat patties. Separate individual portions with 2 sheets of foil or freezer paper so that they can be separated while still frozen. Wrap meat carefully in moisture-vaporproof wrapping, excluding air. Seal and label with the name of the contents, the weight, and the date.

Freeze quickly; store at 0° or below. Do not pack the packages of meat tightly in your freezer because this slows down the freezing process. If you have more than 20 pounds to freeze at once, it is best to have a locker plant freeze it, then transfer it to your home freezer. Hold frozen meat at 0° or below.

A rapid turnover of frozen foods is best. For best quality, use foods within recommended freezer storage time—see chart, page 13.

Cooked foods for the freezer

Effortless meals . . . meals for emergencies . . . meals for "cookless" days. Cooked foods in the freezer mean all of these, and more. They are the "heat and eat" foods that save the day. Here are six fundamental rules to follow in preparing them:

1. Don't oversalt cooked foods—it's better to add more later.
2. Avoid high seasonings.
3. Don't overcook foods to be frozen.
4. Cool quickly before packaging; freeze immediately in meal-size portions.
5. Don't refreeze cooked foods.
6. Use frozen food within recommended storage time—see page 13.

Meat dishes: Roasts, meat loaf, meat stews, and dishes, such as spaghetti sauce and meat balls or corned-beef hash, are good items to freeze. If roasts are whole, wrap securely in foil or other moisture-vaporproof wrapping and tie in stockinet. Slices of roast meat should be frozen with a protective covering of gravy. Package other foods *after they have cooled*, in meal-size cartons. Do not overcook foods to be frozen.

Creamed dishes: If cream sauces and gravies separate after freezing, beat with a fork or spoon during reheating. Separation is usually caused by the combination of fat and the flour used as thickener. So for creamed dishes (such as chicken) and a la kings, use fat sparingly when making sauce.

Sandwiches, appetizers, and fillings: Sandwiches ready to go right in the lunch box (they will be thawed by eating time) are so handy. Do not put "fresh" foods such as lettuce, chopped celery, or sliced tomatoes in sandwiches. Thinly butter both sides of sandwich to keep bread from getting soggy; or spread one side with mustard, softened cream cheese, or salad dressing. No jelly fillings, mayonnaise, or hard-cooked egg whites should be used.

Wrap the sandwiches in moisture-vaporproof wrapping and seal tightly. Place wrapped sandwiches in plastic container.

Other cooked foods that freeze well: Chop suey and soups of all kinds. To save freezer space, freeze concentrated meat stock.

How to freeze meats, poultry, and fish

	Preparation for freezing	How to thaw and cook
MEAT (general)	Avoid packing more bone than necessary. Wrap tightly in moisture-vaporproof material, separating individual portions with 2 layers of waxed or freezer paper. Seal, label, and date. Freeze quickly.	Thaw, wrapped, in refrigerator. If cooked without thawing, allow 12 to 25 minutes extra *per pound* of meat.
POULTRY	Wrap giblets separately; insert in cavity. Never freeze stuffed poultry. Wrap bird snugly in moisture-vaporproof wrapping. Seal and label. Freeze quickly.	Thaw, wrapped, in refrigerator. Or, if in a sealed package, poultry may be defrosted under cold running water.
FISH AND SEA FOOD	Freeze fish immediately or refrigerate overnight. Clean and wash. Wrap in moisture-vaporproof wrapping. To glaze whole fish, freeze on baking sheet. Warm to loosen and dip into ice water. Let ice film freeze. A second dipping will thicken the ice coating formed. Wrap carefully. Seal, label, and freeze. *Crabs, lobsters, shrimp:* Cook as for eating. Cool quickly. Remove meat from shell. Package and freeze. Or freeze shrimp raw, removing heads. Tip: Freeze shrimp on baking sheet; store in plastic container.	Thaw partially in original wrapping in refrigerator, or cook frozen—use a lower cooking temperature than for fresh fish. Thaw, wrapped, only enough to break apart.

How to freeze prepared and cooked foods

	Preparation for freezing	How to thaw and cook
MEAT Meat dishes	*Meat loaf and meat balls, chop suey, corned-beef hash, Spanish rice:* Do not overcook. Cool quickly to room temperature. Pack in freezer containers in meal-size amounts. For liquid foods, allow head space. Seal tightly, label, and date. Freeze immediately.	Heat over low heat, in top of double boiler, or in casserole in oven.
Roast meat	Leave cooked meat in large compact pieces whenever possible. Wrap snugly, forcing out air, in moisture-vaporproof wrapping. Freeze. If you freeze small pieces, hold flavor by covering them with gravy or sauce; package and freeze.	*Frozen dry:* Thaw, wrapped, in refrigerator. Serve cold or reheat. *Frozen in sauce:* Reheat in double boiler, in covered casserole in oven, or in saucepan over low heat.
Beef and veal stews	Use ingredients of highest quality. Omit potatoes. Shorten cooking time. Cook quickly and package.	Heat in casserole or foilware pan in oven, or in top of double boiler.
POULTRY Creamed dishes	Almost any type of creamed dish freezes except those containing hard-cooked egg white. Avoid overcooking. Cool rapidly by floating in pan of ice water. Package in wide-mouth freezer containers. Freeze.	Put in top of double boiler; heat through. Or heat and stir over low heat.
Roast poultry	Same as roast meat.	Same as roast meat.
FISH	Prepare and cook fish dishes as usual. Some that freeze well include fish a la king, fish in cheese sauce, fish and rice, fish hash, fish chowder, fish in creole sauce, lobster thermidor. Cool quickly and freeze.	Heat and serve.
SOUPS	Some soups that freeze well are meat stock, split pea, navy bean, French onion. Cool quickly by floating in pan of ice water. Package, seal, and freeze.	Thaw cream soups in double boiler, clear soups in a saucepan over low heat. Heat to serving temperature.

It's barbecue time!

Charcoal favorite— beef
sizzle a steak!

A cookout is special when you broil steak. Choose from this big roundup—club steak to sirloin. Try them all for variety

1 *Top loin steak* is boneless. Other names: strip, Kansas City, New York steak.

2 *T-bone* boasts tenderloin. T-bone with a big tenderloin is called a Porterhouse.

3 *Club steak* has rib bone along side. No tenderloin, but plenty good.

4 *Top sirloin steak* (boneless) is a snap to carve, makes 2 or 3 servings.

5 *Rib-eye steak* is boneless. Another good bet to barbecue: Thick tenderloin slices.

6 *Blade or chuck steak* from first two ribs of chuck is tender enough to grill.

Slash fat edge at intervals to keep steaks flat. (Choose steaks at least 1¼ inches thick —these are popular strip steaks. Remove meat from refrigerator an hour before grilling, so it's at *room temperature*.) When coals are hot as blazes, tap off ash with fire tongs. Let grill heat; grease with suet. On with the steaks!

Ready to turn? Yes, when you see little bubbles on top. Heat forces the juices to the un-cooked surface. Flip steaks with tongs and turn-er. Piercing with fork wastes those precious juices. Broil second side less long than first— turn only once. For medium-rare, allow about 14 to 18 minutes *total* broiling time.

Rare orders go on last. Some chefs like to salt and pepper each browned side right after turning; others season steaks as they come from the grill. If you go for steak with that deep-

brown, crusty coat and char flavor, here's how: Sear one side by lowering grill close to coals for 2 or 3 minutes, then raise grill to finish same side; turn steak, repeat for second side.

At your next *outdoor barbecue*
treat the gang to pork
over the coals

A whiff of barbecued pork
in the air—no need to call folks
for supper. They come!

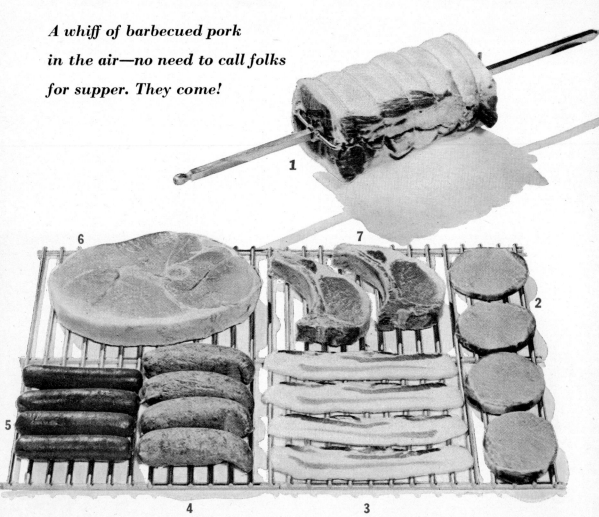

Can't beat barbecued pork for flavor! These cuts are grill specials

1 *Boneless loin*—kingpin of fresh pork. Easy carving! Here two loins are tied together to serve the crowd. Roast on spit, or smoke-cook.

2 *Canadian-style bacon.* Broil slices on foil, or roast a whole roll on the rotisserie.

3 *Bacon strips*—broil thick slices on foil.

4 *Smoked sausage links.* Prick; grill till well done. In a rush? Use brown-and-serves.

5 *Frankfurters.* Score in corkscrew fashion. Put 'em across the grill for zebra stripes.

6 *Center ham slice* (1 to 2 inches thick) gets a flavor finale of glaze and hickory on the brazier at right. Buy fully cooked ham for grill.

7 *Pork rib chops.* Lock these 1-inchers in a rotisserie basket and let 'er roll above slow coals till well done. Or roast on a covered grill.

Barbecued Ribs on a Spit—full of outdoor flavor! Lace loin-back ribs (they're the extra meaty kind) on rotisserie, accordion style. Let rotate over *slow* coals 1 hour or till meat is well done (no pink when you snip between bones). Last 15 minutes, toss damp hickory on coals and baste meat well with Revved-up Rib Sauce or 1-2-3 Sauce (page 156), or Warren's Barbecue Sauce.

Grill-glazed Ham Slices. Gentle heat gives ham a tantalizing brown, yet keeps it moist and tender. About 10 to 15 minutes on each side does the trick because you start with fully cooked ham. Few minutes before serving, swish with this glaze: Heat ½ cup syrup from spiced crab apples with 1 cup brown sugar. Grill partners are crab apples in remaining glaze, hominy in sour cream.

It's *barbecue time!* Cook up fun and good eating with lamb —and kabob stunts

Enjoy old-world lamb barbecues—flavor plus!

1 *Loin chops*—choicest cut! Serve lamb *hot.*

2 *Patties,* girdled with bacon, keep moist.

3 *Kabobs.* Boneless lamb cut from leg.

4 *Shoulder chops.* Arm chop, left, and blade chop, right, are grill bargains. Rub with pressed garlic or French dressing.

5 *Sirloin chops*—meaty. Best pink inside.

6 *Rib chops.* Grill 2-inchers—no drying out.

7 *Saratoga chops*—cut from shoulder, skewered in rounds, centered with kidney slice.

Kabob string-ups! Here's the rundown from top: Whole tomatoes and little patty-pan squashes; your choice of Lamb Teriyaki; Hawaiian Ham on a Stick; Shashlik (lamb marinated in herb sauce); Husky Beef Kabobs. Recipes on pages 156, 157, 158. Broil at a brisk pace for juicy meat, luscious browning.

For out-of-this-world
barbecue flavor, try rotisserie roasting

Pick your cut of meat, rotate it on the spit—something terrific happens! One taste and you'll be a rotisserie-roasting fan for life!

Spin these cuts on the spit; meats baste themselves—delicious

1 *Beef rolled rump*—it's the tantalizing roast on the spit at the right. A best buy!

2 *Lamb rolled shoulder*—thrifty feasting! Or try leg of lamb—so good with garlic inserted. Push spit in at angle to balance uneven roasts.

3 *Smoked boneless rolled ham* is fully cooked. See rotisserie directions, page 47.

4 *Boneless Boston butt*—a penny-wise roast!

5 *Beef rib-eye roast.* Top of the line, but it's all meat! Others: Rolled rib, standing rib roast.

Store roast in refrigerator before cooking. Slip holding fork on rod. Push rod through *center* of roast, inserting tines of fork firmly into meat. Push in second holding fork; fasten.

Balance test: Cradle ends of rod in your upturned hands and rotate roast. If it twirls evenly, fine! If not, then it's off center. Better remount and test again—or add counterbalances to adjust weight.

Tighten fork screws with pliers. A meat thermometer is only trusty guide for doneness. Insert so tip is in center of roast, not touching fat, bone, or metal spit.

A magnificent roast, this beef rolled rump! Now it's cooked to the doneness you like—See Rotisserie Roasting directions on page 158. If you let the roast firm up about 20 minutes before carving, it will slice beautifully; keep it rotating, but lower firebox so cooking stops. Easy go-withs: Baked potatoes, corn on the cob, tossed salad.

Stretch your budget at *barbecue time* with penny-wise meat

How to shape up hamburger

1 *Little meat balls*—cook in long-handled pan, or corral in foilware pan.
2 *Mile-high Burgers.* Stack burgers with cheese slices between. Recipe, page 157.
3 *Olive Treasure-burgers*—filled with cheese and ripe olives. Recipe, page 157.
4 *Wagon wheel.* Pat out 1½ pounds ground beef in circle. Mark 6 spokes, grill in broil basket. Each pioneer gets a wedge.
5 *Donuts.* Hole's for catsup, mustard.
6 *Square cuts.* Pat out a big rectangle of ground beef; cut in strips, then across.
7 *Beef logs.* Make 'em to fit coney buns.

No plain fare here! Reach for a Filet Buckaroo, front of grill. Sure, it's that same old favorite, minute steak—but different. It's spread with mustard, rolled around dill pickle, broiled. Fabulous flavor. Recipe, page 157.

Have a Wiener-kraut, too (left). Franks are filled with tomato-y kraut, wrapped in bacon strips, then grilled to a turn. Recipe, page 158.

Barbecue bargains

1. **Pork blade roast—**an economical cut from the loin. Cook on rotisserie till well done.
2. **Lamb riblets.** Every bite's a treat. Follow recipe on page 56—but cook outdoors.
3. **Minute steaks.** Roll up for Filets Buckaroo.
4. **Beef blade steak.** Turn it into our Silver-plated Pot Roast.
5. **Beef short ribs.** Trim fat; use tenderizer. Broil over hot coals with hickory 25 to 30 minutes; turn often—will be rare.
6. **Beef fresh boneless brisket.** Smoke-cook *slowly* about 4 hours. Slice *thin;* in foilware pan, cover slices with barbecue sauce. Heat slowly 1 hour in smoker.
7. **Lamb barbecue ribs**—a new cut, meatier than pork spareribs. Cook like riblets.

Silver-plated Pot Roast. Snip open the foil package and whiff the mouth-watering aroma of beef browned over hickory, then wrapped up to cook with onions, carrots, green-pepper rings, tomato. It's a specialty just as much as a bigwig cut of meat. With it serve French-bread toast, fruit platter.

You can double your *grill-cooking* repertoire with hickory-barbecuing

These cuts take well to hickory. See "Smoke Memo," page 158

1 *Pork spareribs.* If you can cook with indirect heat on your covered smoker, lay the whole slab on grill—no need to turn. Otherwise, have cut for rotisserie.

2 *Pork chops*—splendid choice for hood-down cooking. Add hickory early for heavy smoking, toward end for light touch. Tops in chops are the loin cuts at left; rib chops, right.

3 *Pork boneless loin strip.* Smoke-barbecue on rotisserie or grill. No pink when done.

4 *Broiler-fryer halves.* Put chicks bone side down on grill. Be gentle with smoking.

5 *Pork back ribs* are extra-meaty ribs.

6 *Leg of lamb.* Most folks like just a faint overtone of smoke flavor with lamb, so go easy at first. Spit-roast.

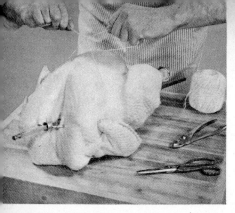  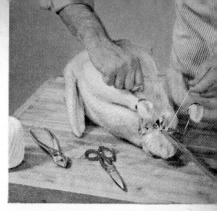

Rub inside of bird with 2 table-spoons salt. Skewer neck skin to back. Facing breast, insert spit at angle to avoid bone. Anchor with holding forks fore and aft. Check balance.

Loop long piece of cord over right wing, loop around skewer, then over left wing to hold *flat;* tie (first picture). Wrap cord around turkey just above "elbows" and tie again. Tie all again for firm bundle.

This big bird has a drum-stick holding fork to let heat reach inside thigh meat. Tie tail to rod; if you don't have "brace-lets," cross legs, tie to rod, too.

Toss on chips for best-ever turkey! Brush with salad oil. Roast with hood down, slow coals at back of barbecue, a drip pan under revolving bird. Replenish hickory now and then. Takes about 12 to 15 minutes *per pound*. Test for done-ness (page 88). Meat thermometer in the thigh should read 195°. For easier carving, let turkey rest 15 minutes.

Here's barbecue how-to—outdoors, everyone!

Kabob Tips

Speedy marinade: Add rosemary or other favorite herb to oil-vinegar or Italian dressing—bottled or from salad-dressing mix.

Dandy kabob tidbits: Try canned whole onions, canned potatoes, pitted ripe olives, stuffed green olives, bacon strips, gherkins, canned pineapple chunks, or canned peach halves. Baste the vegetables and fruits with melted butter or margarine while broiling.

Do green peppers and mushrooms fall apart in skewering? First give them a boiling water bath for a minute. Or use an ice pick to make small hole first.

To avoid overcooking, string vegetables, such as tomatoes, on their own skewer.

Shashlik

2 pounds boneless lamb, cut in
  1½-inch cubes

• • •

Rosemary Marinade or Armenian Herb
  Marinade

• • •

Kabob tidbits: Quartered green peppers,
  quartered sweet red peppers, onions,
  cut in thirds, other favorites to suit
  yourself

Add lamb cubes to marinade and stir to coat. Let refrigerate overnight or stand at room temperature 2 or 3 hours, turning meat occasionally. Fill 6 skewers, alternating meat cubes with vegetables. Broil over hot coals to medium rare, brushing often with melted butter or margarine. (Use rotating skewers or turn often on grill.)

Rosemary Marinade: Combine ¼ cup each salad oil and wine vinegar, 2 teaspoons each salt and crushed rosemary, ½ teaspoon pepper, and ½ cup sliced onion. Use to marinate lamb or chicken. Enough for 1½ to 2 pounds meat.

Armenian Herb Marinade: Combine ½ cup olive or salad oil, ¼ cup lemon juice, 1 teaspoon each salt, marjoram, and thyme, 1 clove garlic, minced, ½ cup chopped onion, and ¼ cup snipped parsley. Use to marinate lamb or chicken. Enough for 1½ to 2 pounds meat.

Teriyaki—Beef or Lamb

Follow recipe for Shashlik, but use tender beef or lamb, and *Teriyaki Marinade:* Combine ⅔ cup soy sauce, ¼ cup salad oil, 2 tablespoons molasses, 2 teaspoons monosodium glutamate, 2 teaspoons ginger or 2 tablespoons grated ginger root, 2 teaspoons dry mustard, and 6 cloves garlic, minced. Makes enough for 2 pounds meat.

Revved-up Rib Sauce

1 cup extra-hot catsup
½ cup water
¼ cup molasses
¼ cup vinegar
3 tablespoons Worcestershire
  sauce
2 teaspoons salt
½ teaspoon dry mustard
¼ teaspoon freshly ground pepper
2 cloves garlic, minced

Mix ingredients well and let stand to mellow at least a few hours. Give sauce a good stir just before using.

You'll like the punch of this sauce on burgers, too.

1-2-3 Sauce

1 bottle extra-hot catsup
2 teaspoons celery seed
3 tablespoons garlic vinegar or wine
  vinegar

Mix ingredients. Taste. Like more seasoning? Do as you please. Use to baste loin back or spareribs the last 15 minutes of spit-barbecuing. Makes about 1¼ cups.

Cran-burger Sauce

1 1-pound can (2 cups) jellied
  cranberry sauce
⅓ cup meat sauce
1 tablespoon brown sugar
1 tablespoon salad oil
2 teaspoons prepared mustard

Combine ingredients and beat with electric or rotary beater (or blend in blender). Serve as is or heat; smear on hot-from-the-grill burgers, or on ham.

Makes about 2 cups.

Hawaiian Ham on a Stick

String 2-inch squares of boneless fully cooked ham on skewers along with quarters of pineapple. (See picture on page 149). While broiling over slow coals, brush pineapple with butter or margarine, and the ham with Honey Glaze, page 45.

West Coast Tomato Sauce

½ cup chopped onion
1 8-ounce can (1 cup) seasoned tomato
　　sauce
1 cup water
½ cup catsup
2 tablespoons brown sugar
2 tablespoons prepared mustard
1 tablespoon salad oil
1 tablespoon Worcestershire sauce
Few drops Tabasco sauce

Combine all ingredients. Cover; simmer slowly till onion is tender, about 30 minutes. Makes about 2 cups.

Make ahead; keep in covered jar in refrigerator, all set to go.

Silver-plated Pot Roast

4 pounds blade-bone pot roast,
　　1½ inches thick
　　　　•　•　•
3 tablespoons enriched flour
1 tablespoon brown sugar
1 teaspoon salt
Dash pepper
½ teaspoon dry mustard
¾ cup catsup
1½ tablespoons Worcestershire
　　sauce
1 tablespoon vinegar
　　　　•　•　•
1 or 2 stalks celery, sliced on bias
6 small whole carrots
2 medium onions, quartered
1 medium green pepper, cut in rings
2 firm medium tomatoes, in wedges

Brown roast slowly on grill over hot coals with hickory added, about 20 to 30 minutes. Season well with salt and pepper. Combine next 8 ingredients for sauce. Tear off 5-foot length of household-weight foil; fold double (or use 2½ feet heavy-duty foil). Spoon *half* of sauce in center of foil. Place meat atop and cover with vegetables and remaining sauce. Fold foil over and seal securely; bake over slow coals 1½ to 2 hours or till tender. Makes 6 servings.

Olive Treasure-burgers

1 pound ground beef*
¼ cup chopped ripe olives
¼ cup shredded sharp process
　　American cheese
　　　　•　•　•
Salt and pepper

Divide meat in fourths. Using a 5-inch canister cover as guide, draw a circle on waxed paper. Place a fourth of the meat in center and pat *gently* (or place waxed paper on top, too, and roll *lightly* with rolling pin) to fill circle. Do not press hard.

Now for the filling. Leaving a ½-inch margin for sealing, top half of patty with ripe olives and cheese. Lift corner of waxed paper at the back to fold meat over filling. Press around margin to seal in filling.

Brush patties with salad oil or melted margarine to keep from sticking to grill. Broil over hot coals about 12 minutes, turning once. Dash with salt and pepper. Pass bowl of barbecue sauce. Makes 4 servings.

Note: If meat is lean, have 2 or 3 ounces of suet ground with each pound. Meat will be juicier and more tender.

Filets Buckaroo

Flatten minute steaks and spread one side lightly with prepared mustard. At narrow end of each, place a strip of dill pickle or candied dill pickle, or 1 or 2 green onions. Roll up, starting at end with pickle. Fasten with small metal skewers or toothpicks; brush outside with melted margarine. Broil on grill over hot coals about 10 to 15 minutes, turning once. When done to your liking, season with salt and pepper.

Mile-high Burgers

For each person, pat out a 4-inch ground-beef patty; a 3-inch patty; and a 2-inch patty—all a little over ½ inch thick. Place on greased grill or spread both sides of patties with soft butter or margarine. Salt and pepper top side. Broil over hot coals about 5 minutes, turn and broil 3 minutes more or till done to your liking. Season.

Now for the stacking: giant burger, round of sharp process American cheese; middle-size patty, middle-size cheese slice; midget burger. Top with cheese or olive; drive wooden skewer through all.

Smoke Memo

Don't miss out on the flavor-plus of hickory. For adjustment of firebox and draft, and for cooking times, check directions that come with your equipment. Wait till charcoal burns down to low heat before adding hickory. (Soak hunks, crosscuts, or bark in water 1 hour; dampen sawdust or flakes when you start the fire.)

Hickory-barbecuing requires a smoke cooker with full hood, charcoal oven, or Chinese oven. The cooking is long, the heat indirect (charcoal fire, almost hickory-smothered, at one end, food at other). With some grills you smoke-cook directly over the fire with barbecue closed. Some equipment permits both methods and rotisserie smoke-barbecuing in addition.

Open grill "smoking"—toss on damp hickory toward end of cooking time.

Brush-on "smoking"—for hurry-up or indoors. Before cooking, brush the burgers, franks, or chicken with liquid smoke, or dash with smoked salt. Or add liquid smoke to barbecue sauce.

Mock Filet of Beef

    1 3-pound eye-of-round steak
      2½ to 3 inches thick
    Instant nonseasoned
      meat tenderizer

Sprinkle steak with nonseasoned meat tenderizer according to package directions. Center steak on spit and tie securely with cord. Roast slowly over charcoal on motorized spit about 1½ hours or to desired doneness—use meat thermometer for final judge. During cooking, baste frequently with Warren's Barbecue Sauce (page 138).

To serve, cut thin slices of steak on bias, across the grain; pass extra barbecue sauce. Makes about 8 servings.

Back-yard Barbecued Ribs

Salt loin back ribs; place, bone side down, on grill over *slow* coals. Broil 30 minutes; turn meaty side down till nicely browned. Turn meaty side up again; broil 30 minutes longer. Brush with Warren's Barbecue Sauce (page 138); peg on a few slices of lemon and onion with toothpicks. Broil without turning 30 minutes more or till well done. Allow about 1 pound per person.

Husky Beef Kabobs

For 8 servings, choose 3 pounds lean beef round or chuck, cut in 1½-inch cubes. Add beef cubes to California Marinade, turning to coat. Refrigerate 24 to 36 hours to give marinade time to tenderize the beef; turn the meat occasionally. Fill skewers, alternating meat cubes with mushroom caps or other kabob tidbits of your choice. Broil over hot coals to rare or medium rare, brushing frequently with melted butter or margarine. (Use rotating skewers or turn often on grill.)

California Marinade: Mix 1 cup salad oil, ¾ cup soy sauce, ½ cup lemon juice, ¼ cup each Worcestershire sauce and prepared mustard, 1 to 2 teaspoons coarsely cracked pepper, and 2 cloves garlic, minced.

Wiener-krauts

Slit wieners lengthwise to about ¼ inch from each end. Toss drained sauerkraut with a sprinkle of caraway seed and a little catsup. Stuff wieners with mixture; wrap each with a bacon strip, anchoring ends with toothpicks. Broil over hot coals, turning once, till bacon is crisp.

Rotisserie Roasting

Insert spit rod following directions on page 151. Arrange hot coals at back of firebox, a drip pan in front under roast. Knock gray ash from coals. Attach spit, turn on motor, and cook till meat thermometer says "when"—see temperatures, back cover.

Grill-broiled Chicken

    2 ready-to-cook young chickens (about
      2 pounds each), split in half
      lengthwise

So birds will stay flat during broiling, break joints of drumstick, hip, and wing. Let chicken refrigerate in Out-West Marinade at least 4 or 5 hours, turning occasionally. Place on grill with bone side or inside nearest the coals. Broil slowly. When well browned, 20 to 30 minutes, turn skin side down and cook about 30 minutes longer or till tender, brushing occasionally with marinade. Makes 4 servings.

Out-West Marinade: Combine 1 envelope Italian (or garlic-cheese) salad-dressing mix and ¼ cup lemon juice. Add ½ cup salad oil.

Index